Friday the 13th Trivia

By

Lelia Moncure Koval

ISBN: 1-4033-3121-9 (e-book)
ISBN: 1-4033-3122-7 (Paperback)

This book is printed on acid free paper.

1stBooks – rev. 06/26/03

I'd like to dedicate this book to my dad, Smiley, who was the one responsible for getting me hooked on the Friday The 13th movies 13 years ago and has been an inspiration to me over the years.

Dad, Thank You for your support and believing in me.

Love Lelia

Friday the 13th (Part 1) Trivia Questions

A.   **Matching: Match the actors or actresses with the character they portrayed.**

1.	Peter Brouwer	A. Annie
2.	Adrienne King	B. Crazy Ralph
3.	Mark Nelson	C. Truck Driver
4.	Betsy Palmer	D. Claudette
5.	Ari Lehman	E. Barry
6.	Rex Everhart	F. Pamela Voorhees
7.	Robbi Morgan	G. Bill
8.	Kevin Bacon	H. Alice
9.	Walt Gorney	I. Brenda
10.	Ron Carroll	J. Marcie
11.	Ron Milkie	K. Ned
12.	Laurie Bartram	L. Jack
13.	Harry Crosby	M. Jason Voorhees
14.	Jeannine Taylor	N. Officer Dorf
15.	Willie Adams	O. Sgt. Tierney
16.	Debra S. Hayes	P. Steve Christy

B.   **Questions: Answer the questions about the movie.**

17.   Who decapitated Jason's vengeful mother?
18.   Because of the killings Camp Crystal Lake was called what?
19.   Who was the first person to get killed?
20.   How many people were killed?
21.   Who survived?
22.   Who turned out to be the killer at the end of the movie?
23.   Who played Jason?
24.   How was Steve Christy killed?
25.   What happened to Alice at the end of the movie?
26.   What gave you the clue that Mrs. Voorhees was the killer?
27.   Who was the owner of Camp Crystal Lake?
28.   How did Jack die?

29.   Who tried to warn Annie to stay away from Camp Crystal Lake?

30.   What was the reason that was given to stay away from Camp Crystal Lake?

31.   Who never reached the camp?

32.   Why?

33.   What was the actual month and day that all of this started?

34.   What year did a young boy drown?

35.   What was the name of the young boy?

36.   What was his mother doing at the camp the day that he drowned?

37.   Who was his mother?

38.   Who was the town drunk that went around warning everybody about Camp Crystal Lake's death curse?

39.   Who played Alice?

40.   Who was the very last person that got killed?

41.   How?

42.   Whose dead body was thrown through a window?

43.   Whose dead body is in Mrs. Voorhees jeep?

44.   Who played Steve Christy?

45.   Who played Mrs. Voorhees?

46.   What was the name of the truck driver that gave Annie a ride?

47.   What color vehicle gave Annie a ride before she got killed?

48.   What was the name of the sheriff?

49.   Who played the truck driver?

50.   Who played Annie?

51.   Who played Jack?

52.   Who played Ned?

53.   Who played Bill?

54.   Who played Marcie?

55.   Who played Brenda?

56.   What was the weather like when Steve Christy was in the diner drinking a cup of coffee?

57.   Where was the movie filmed?

58.   Name the bloopers

59.   Name the cut scenes.

60.   Name in order the people and how they were killed.

61.   Who played Sgt. Tierney?

About the Author

Larry Hall was born in Dalton Georgia and resides there today. He Has a Bachelors Degree in Psychology and a Masters and Doctorate in Computer Science. He has been married to Sharon West Hall for twenty-five years. They have four children and four grandchildren and another on the way. He is a self-proclaimed computer geek, gourmet chef and photographer. He has worked as a meter reader, forklift operator, railroad bridge engineer, heavy machine operator, union carpenter, studio musician and wedding photographer as well as a computer consultant and programmer for the past nineteen years. He has written technical articles for various computer magazines and periodicals as well as spoken at various computer seminars and conventions around the country.

62. Who were the three people that arrived together?
63. Who was the person that found a snake in the cabin?
64. When she screamed, who came running?
65. Who killed the snake?
66. What did he use to kill the snake?
67. In one point of the movie, you notice the killer was wearing a ring, which hand was she wearing it on and which finger?
68. When Jason came out of the water and pulled Alice under he was covered in something, what was it?
69. What do the people in town refer to Camp Crystal Lake as?
70. Why?
71. What was the name of the Police officer on the motorcycle?
72. Who faked drowning?
73. How many people were in the diner, when Annie went in?
74. When Jack, Ned and Brenda arrived what did they help Steve Christy with?
75. What was Bill doing?
76. Where was he?
77. What did Alice ask Bill?
78. What did Steve Christy look at of Alice's and told her that she was very good at it?
79. Name all of the things that Alice did to Mrs. Voorhees to try to stop her?
80. How did Mrs. Voorhees introduce herself to Alice?
81. What color was the jeep that Steve Christy had?
82. What color was the jeep that Mrs. Voorhees had?
83. What did Alice use to decapitate Pamela Voorhees?
84. At the end of Part 1, who pulled Alice out of the lake?
85. Who didn't Sgt. Tierney find?
86. Whose dead body fell out of the tree?
87. Who did Ned scare at the Archery Range?
88. Who did Steve Christy get a lift from?
89. Why did he need a lift?
90. What kind of shorts was Steve Christy wearing?
91. Who rescued Ned from drowning?
92. Right before Steve Christy leaves the camp, he looks up at the sky and says something, what did he say?
93. What was Steve Christy doing right before he got killed?

94. Right before Steve Christy got killed, what did he say to the killer?
95. What color of eyes did the killer have?
96. Did Steve Christy make it back to the camp?
97. What was Bill, doing before he got killed?
98. At the beginning of the movie, what did Steve Christy have around his neck?
99. Was he wearing a shirt?
100. What year were Barry and Claudette killed?
101. How many bags does Annie arrive in town with?
102. How many miles is it to Camp Crystal Lake from the restaurant?
103. What phone number is on the side of the truck driver's truck?
104. What's the name of the truck driver?
105. What color was the truck?
106. What does the truck driver warn Annie about the camp?
107. Why does Alice say she might have to go to California?
108. What color shirt does Ned wear?
109. What does Ned have in his arms when he surprised Brenda?
110. Who knocked over the nightstand when Bill was catching the snake to kill it?
111. What did Officer Dorf ask the kids?
112. Who was outside the cabin when Alice screams, after finding the snake?
113. What were Barry and Claudette doing when they were killed?
114. Who is hiding in the pantry?
115. Who does Ralph, startle as she was putting the pans away?
116. What did Officer Dorf say about Crazy Ralph?
117. What do Jack and Marcie do on a log?
118. What nightmare does Marcie tell Jack?
119. What number was on the canoe that rescued Ned?
120. Who was playing the guitar?
121. Where did the killer place Ned's body?
122. Where did Marcie go when she left Jack alone?
123. What game are the counselors playing around the fireplace?
124. Who were playing the game?
125. Who is the banker when they played the game?
126. Who buys Baltic Avenue?

127. Who said, "No one ever lands on Baltic Avenue"
128. Who lands on Baltic Avenue
129. Who bought Kentucky Avenue?
130. What is used to pay rent?
131. Could chance give them their clothes back?
132. Who ended up being the first person to pay rent in the game?
133. Who asks, "What if Steve showed up"?
134. Who said, "he can keep the boots, everything else goes"?
135. How did Jack get murdered?
136. What did Marcie repair in the bathroom?
137. Where did Marcie get killed?
138. How did Marcie get murdered?
139. What is the name of the waitress that waited on Steve?
140. What color was Sandy's hair?
141. What color is Brenda's raincoat?
142. What color was Brenda's flashlight?
143. Who helped Steve with a ride when his jeep broke down?
144. What color is Brenda's nightgown?
145. Why is Brenda out in the rainstorm?
146. Were there any off-screen kills?
147. Why does Brenda scream?
148. Where was Brenda killed?
149. Did Brenda get killed off-screen?
150. What color is the board that Alice breaks the window with?
151. What message came over the police radio?
152. What color was Steve's raincoat?
153. Did Steve Christy wear glasses?
154. Who went into the emergency generator room?
155. Who got killed in the emergency generator room?
156. Who carries a kerosene lamp into the emergency generator room?
157. What does Alice place on the antique gas stove?
158. Where does Alice look for Bill?
159. Did she find him dead?
160. What does Alice do inside the cabin?
161. Whose dead body is thrown through the window cabin?
162. What does Mrs. Voorhees tell Alice?
163. Who said to Officer Dorf, "There are no crazies around here"?

164. What color are Mrs. Voorhees' eyes?
165. What was Mrs. Voorhees wearing when she met Alice?
166. Where was Alice and Mrs. Voorhees when Mrs. Voorhees was beheaded?
167. What did Sgt. Tierney tell Alice in the hospital?
168. When Sgt. Tierney's men pulled Alice out of the lake, did they think that she was dead too?
169. What color was Alice's blanket?
170. What year was the movie filmed and how long was the movie?
171. In the end of the first movie, Why did Jason come out of the lake as a child?
172. What was the name of the cemetery that Enos drops Annie off at?
173. What is Officer Dorf's motorcycle number as stated by the radio?
174. What year was it when the first two people were killed?
175. What year did the movie take place…in the present day?
176. Were there any script differences?
177. Name the script differences.
178. Who was officer Dorf looking for?
179. Why?
180. What were the problems that the camp was faced with when it tried to open up?
181. What year did the camp open up with problems of bad water?
182. Who mentions of these problems?
183. Who does he mention them to?
184. When Bill went to check the emergency generator, what was Alice doing?
185. When Alice wakes up all by herself, who's name did she call out for?
186. Who were the special make-up effects by?
187. Who was the associate producer?
188. Who were the stunts by?
189. What color was the truck that Jack, Marcie and Ned arrived to the camp in?
190. Who was the music by?
191. Was Mrs. Voorhees the cook every year until Jason died?
192. What was her maiden name?

193. When was she born?
194. What was her first name and middle name?
195. Who directed this movie?
196. What was the reason that Betsy Palmer was picked for the role of Mrs. Voorhees?
197. When Harry Manfredini did the music for this movie, where was it done and with what?
198. At the beginning of the movie, name one song that the campers were singing?
199. Name who were killed off-screen?
200. After Bill was murdered, how many people were left?
201. When Annie arrived in town, how many times did the town clock strike?
202. When Annie was in the restaurant, what was the name of the waitress?
203. How long did Enos say that Steve Christy had been working on fixing up the camp?
204. When they showed Marcie, Jack and Ned coming up the road on their way to Camp Crystal Lake, who was driving?
205. When Annie hitched a ride with an unknown stranger, did they miss the turn off for the camp?
206. Did the stranger purposely miss the turn off for the camp?
207. When Annie said "I think we'd better stop"…what did the unknown stranger do?
208. When the driver would not stop, what did Annie do?
209. After Annie gets out of the unknown stranger's jeep, where does Annie go?
210. Did the unknown stranger follow her?
211. What happened to Annie?
212. How?
213. Who played Annie?
214. Who asks, "If you were a flavor of ice cream, what would it be"?
215. Who answered him?
216. What did she say?
217. When Steve Christy gets back to camp in the rain, he passed by a sign…what is written on the sign?
218. What color is the sign?

219. What did Sgt. Tierney ask Alice at the hospital?
220. What did Alice ask Sgt. Tierney?
221. Who is she referring to when she says, "The one who pulled me under the lake"?
222. Who got killed before Mrs.Voorhees was killed?
223. How was he killed?
224. Who played him?
225. What was Steve Christy dragging on the back of his jeep when it broke down?
226. Why did Bill, Marcy and Alice stop playing their board game?
227. When Bill and Alice go to Brenda's cabin, what was in her bed?
228. Where was the second place that they checked for Marcie, Jack, Brenda, and Ned?
229. Who said, "I really think we should call someone"?
230. Who was she saying it to?
231. Why couldn't they call anyone?
232. Did the truck start up?
233. Whose truck was used?
234. How far was it from the camp to the nearest crossroads?
235. What color was Ralph's hat?
236. When Annie jumped from the stranger's jeep, did she hurt herself?
237. What did she hurt?
238. Did the stranger back up the jeep before going after her?
239. Did the stranger go after Annie on foot?
240. How did the stranger kill Annie?
241. Who told Alice that she is very pretty and talented?
242. What did Bill tell Alice that was needed for Steve to get, when Alice asked him about needing more paint?
243. How much money did Steve drop, fixing up the camp?
244. Who gives this info in the movie?
245. Who does he tell it to?
246. Who played the waitress Trudy?
247. What do they only show of the stranger when going after Annie?
248. When Ned, Jack and Marcie arrived, who did Steve yell for?
249. Which cabin did Alice say was all cleaned up?

250. Who was going to be the cook at the camp?
251. How many kids and staff would she be cooking for?
252. Did Enos take Annie half way to camp?
253. What did Trudy call it?
254. Who produced this movie?
255. What was the released date for this movie?
256. What was the film' budget?
257. How much did the film make at the box-office?
258. When was Jason born?
259. What was Jason's dad's full name?
260. How old was Jason when he drowned?
261. When Mrs. Voorhees tells Alice about Jason, did she mention that Jason was her only child?
262. Did Mrs. Voorhees mention that Jason wasn't a good swimmer?
263. Who wore a green shirt with the number 88 on the back, when Bill killed the snake?
264. When Officer Dorf came to the camp, what was Ned wearing?
265. When Officer Dorf came to the camp, who was just getting back from a walk?
266. Who starred in this movie?
267. Did Mrs. Voorhees say this to Alice, "We can go now, dear…it will be easier for you than it was for Jason"?
268. What was Alice's reply?
269. How did Mrs. Voorhees reply to Alice's reply?
270. At the end of the movie, what did Sgt. Tierney tell Alice?
271. What was Alice's reply to what Sgt. Tierney said?
272. Was the stranger that killed Annie, Mrs. Voorhees?
273. When Officer Dorf came to the camp, what kind of vehicle was he driving?
274. Is Harry Crosby, Bing Crosby's son?
275. Who played the boy, Jason?
276. When Annie came to town, what time was announced over the radio?
277. What was the most memorable murder that Ari Lehman remembers?
278. What year was Mrs. Voorhees born?

279. At the end of the movie, when Alice was at the hospital, was she given a shot?
280. As the movie ended, where did the camera pan back to as Alice said, "Then he's still there"?
281. What was the original title given by writer Victor Miller?
282. When was it changed?
283. Why was it changed?
284. Who directed this movie?
285. Who did the special make-up effects?
286. Did he work on any other Friday The 13th movies?
287. What color were Steve Christy's eyes?
288. Whose dead body is in Mrs. Voorhee's jeep?
289. Whose dead body was hanging upside down from a tree?
290. Whose dead body was thrown through a window into a cabin?
291. Who was pinned to a door with arrows?

Friday the 13th (Part 2) Trivia Questions

A. Matching: Match the actors or actresses with the character they portrayed.

1. Jack Marks	A. Alice
2. Marla Kober	B. Scott
3. Stu Charno	C. Ginny
4. Warrington Gillette	D.Crazy Ralph
5. Bill Randolph	E. Vicki
6. John Furey	F. Jason Stunt Double
7. Tom McBride	G. Mrs. Voorhees
8. Amy Steel	H. Jeff
9. Walt Gorney	I. Terri
10. Lauren Marie Taylor	J. The Prowler
11. Adrienne King	K The Cop
12. Jerry Wallace	L. Max
13. Kirsten Baker	M. Paul
14. Russell Todd	N. Ted
15. Steve Daskawitz	O. Sandra
16. Betsy Palmer	P. Jason Voorhees
17. Cliff Cudney	Q. Mark

B. Questions: Answer the following questions about the movie.

18. Who was the first person to get killed?
19. How?
20. When did Alice wake up from her dream...(right after what part)?
21. What color was Alice's cat?
22. How many times did someone call Alice on the phone?
23. How long had it been, since the murders at Camp Crystal Lake, when Alice got killed?
24. At the beginning of the movie, what was the rhyme that the child was singing?
25. What was in Alice's refrigerator?

26. Who called Alice on the phone?
27. What was Alice about to do when she got killed?
28. What was Alice's dream that she had?
29. What scares her, as she was investigating noises from an open window?
30. What room were her drawings in?
31. Who were her drawings of?
32. When she opened her refrigerator, did she scream at the sight of Mrs. Voorhees decapitated head?
33. Who played Jason?
34. How many long years since the killings at Camp Blood and since then Jason had been drowned?
35. Who were the two people that were nosing around Camp Crystal Lake after they were told that it was off limits? (They didn't get too far when they were caught by the cop.)
36. Who was late getting to the counselor training camp?
37. Why?
38. Why was Mark in a wheelchair?
39. How did Mark get killed?
40. Who was the town drunk that went around warning everybody about Camp Crystal Lake?
41. What happened to Crazy Ralph?
42. How?
43. What was he doing when he got killed?
44. Name the cut scenes?
45. Name the bloopers?
46. Who fought with Jason?
47. Who brought their little dog with them?
48. What was the little dog's name?
49. How did the cop get killed?
50. Where was the cop when he got killed?
51. What did the cop say as he was looking in the room, right before Jason killed him?
52. Where did this movie take place?
53. Who stayed behind instead of going out to a bar for a last night out?
54. Who was in charge of the Counselors Training Camp?
55. Who went out for a last night out, to a bar?

56. Who returned from the bar back to the camp?
57. Who called Alice on the phone?
58. Where did Ginny hit Jason, when Paul and Him were fighting?
59. What did she hit him with?
60. What happened near the end of the movie?
61. When Jeff and Sandra got into town…who played a prank on them?
62. What was the prank?
63. When Ginny was hiding from Jason (and Jason was in the same cabin), what did she see to frighten her?
64. When she got frightened, what did she do?
65. Did Jason figure out that she was hiding in that cabin?
66. Where was Jason hiding, when she came out from her hiding place?
67. What weapon was he holding?
68. Did the chair break that he was standing on?
69. Did the Pitchfork break in two pieces?
70. What was the reason for Paul's disappearance?
71. What did Jason wear over his head to cover his face?
72. Who went bar hopping and never came back to the counselor training camp?
73. How many years had passed since the killings at Camp Crystal Lake?
74. When do you get to see Jason's deformed face?
75. What was Ginny's last name?
76. When Terri goes skinny-dipping, who grabs her clothes?
77. What happened to Scott?
78. When Jeff and Sandra, were wandering around the woods in the Camp Crystal Lake area, what did they find?
79. What was the legend of Camp Crystal Lake?
80. In the oldest cabin in Crystal Lake, deep in the woods, what did Jason have in one of the rooms?
81. What was Paul's last name?
82. Who did Ginny pretend to be, to try to fool Jason?
83. What did she have to put on to play the part in trying to fool Jason?
84. Who unmasks Jason?
85. How?

86. What does Paul say after seeing Jason's face?
87. When Ginny was in her car, what did Jason use to try to kill her?
88. When she thought Jason was gone from her cabin, she comes out of her hiding place and where was Jason?
89. What happened?
90. In the cabin what did Ginny attack Jason with?
91. When did it start raining in this movie?
92. When did it start storming?
93. What did Vicki go to the car for?
94. Whose dead body did Vicki see right before she died?
95. Whose name was she calling before she got killed?
96. How was she killed?
97. Whose body did Jason drag down the stairs?
98. Who said, "Nice night" as Paul and Ginny drove up in the Volkswagon?
99. Who said, "Yeah, if you're a duck"?
100. Was there a full Moon?
101. How many different times did Paul and Jason fight?
102. What did Jeff and Ted have to move that was in the middle of the road?
103. Did Ginny's plan work to fool Jason?
104. What did Jason hurt her with?
105. Where?
106. Near the beginning of the movie who did Crazy Ralph warn?
107. What did Sandra find, when Ted and Jeff were moving the log from the middle of the road?
108. At the beginning of the movie, what were Jeff and Sandra doing when Crazy Ralph warned them?
109. What does Crazy Ralph say to Jeff and Sandra?
110. How was Jeff and Sandra punished for going into the Camp Crystal Lake area, when it was off limits?
111. At the bar, who said, "What if the legend is true"?
112. Who told Ginny that she was drunk?
113. Did Jason ever go to school?
114. Who was his only friend?
115. Did he see his mom decapitated?
116. Did he know about death until that horrible night?

117. Who told Ginny, "It's just a legend"?
118. How many off-screen kills were there?
119. At the beginning of the movie who did Ginny pass, that was standing on the side of the road?
120. When the cop leaves his car to chase Jason, what did he forget to do?
121. How did Sandra and Jeff get killed?
122. In the scene, when Paul was telling about the Legend, how many people were gathered around the campfire?
123. What is the name of the camp?
124. What was the name of the bar that Paul, Ginny, Ted and a few others went to for their "Last night out"?
125. What was the name of the band that played in the bar?
126. What was the license plate number of Jeff's truck?
127. What color was Jeff's truck?
128. What was the name of the store that Crazy Ralph stands in front of when he make his first appearance in Part 2?
129. What does Paul state about the area that surrounds the area of Crystal Lake?
130. Who played Ginny?
131. What color was Vicki's car?
132. How many candles surround Jason's mother's head in her shrine?
133. What gas station was near where Jeff and Sandra made their call to Ted?
134. Around the campfire, what did Paul tell everybody?
135. Right, as Paul was finishing up with telling about the Legend of Jason Voorhees, who jumps out and scares everybody?
136. What was he wearing?
137. What was he holding in one hand?
138. In which hand was he holding the spear?
139. Who actually had the idea to sneak over and see "Camp Blood"?
140. What happened during a fight scene when they were first filming Part 2?
141. Who played the Jason stunt double?

142. When Jason and Paul were fighting in the old cabin, Ginny picked up a machete to hit Jason with in the shoulder, whose dead body was lying near the machete, that you see?
143. What parts of the movie were showed in slow motion?
144. What color was Terri's little dog?
145. What is everybody doing when Jeff and Sandra sneak over to "Camp Blood"?
146. Who tells the first riddle?
147. What is the riddle?
148. What is the answer?
149. What riddle does Ted ask?
150. What is the answer?
151. When the cop left his car to chase after someone, who is he chasing after?
152. When Ginny goes into the oldest cabin, and she turns around and looks, who was right outside the cabin?
153. Where did she hide?
154. What weapon did Jason have, when he was breaking the door down?
155. When Ginny went in the room where Jason's mother's head was…did she scream after seeing it?
156. Who directed this movie?
157. Who was the producer of this movie?
158. Who was the stunt coordinator?
159. Who was the music by?
160. When was this movie released?
161. How many re-edits did the film had to go through in order to get the "R" rating?
162. Who did the Special Make-up effects?
163. Who distributed the movie?
164. Was this the last F-13 to be shot at a real camp?
165. How much money was made at the box office?
166. How long was this movie?
167. Before Jason smashed through the window, what was Ginny holding?
168. Who starred in this movie?
169. What was the most memorable murder that Warrington Gillette remembered?

170. Whose murder was that?
171. When do you notice that Ginny takes off the sweater that belonged to Jason's mother?
172. For the filming of this movie, what did Warrington Gillette say the turn-ons were?
173. For the filming of this movie, what did Warrington Gillette say the turn-offs were?
174. Right after Alice got killed, what did Jason remove off of the stove?
175. When Ginny and Paul, got back from the bar, when she realized that they weren't the only ones in the cabin, how did she tell Paul?
176. What happened at the end of the movie?
177. Who survived?
178. Name in order, everyone who was killed and how they were killed.
179. When Jason smashed through the window, what was Ginny holding?
180. What was Paul holding?
181. Who disappeared at the end of the movie and was presumed dead?
182. Who was at the door, right before Jason smashed through the window?
183. What did Alice do right after she wakes up from her dream?
184. Where was this movie filmed?
185. Did Cliff Cudney have a part in this movie?
186. Who did he play?
187. Who were the Special Make-up effects by?
188. After production ended, why did Warrington Gillette complain?
189. Did Jason have a hockey mask in this movie?
190. When Ginny is carried away; by the paramedics, whom does she call out for?
191. How many empty beer bottles did Ted have in front of him at the bar?
192. What does Ginny say about Jason's mother's revenge?
193. At the bar, who said that Jason is just a legend?
194. Who in this movie died in 1992 from Aids?

195.   Who did he play?
196.   Who did Mark say he was sharing a cabin with?
197.   Who was Vicki sharing a cabin with?
198.   Before Vicki runs out to her car, does she turn off her cabin light?
199.   Who used a chainsaw to cut wood?
200.   Did she put it away?
201.   Who was fixing hotdogs for lunch?
202.   Who was Terri looking for when she was called for lunch?
203.   Where did Jason put all of the dead bodies of the victims?
204.   What year was it filmed?
205.   Did the film open up to terrible reviews?
206.   How much money did the movie make at the box-office?
207.   Was the bar that was used in a couple of scenes in the film in town?
208.   Name the places where Paul and Jason fought.
209.   Who went skinny-dipping all alone?
210.   At the bar, who told Ginny she was drunk?
211.   Was it a full moon, when Terri was skinny-dipping?
212.   Who played the extra counselor?
213.   Whose dead body did Vicki see before she died?
214.   What is Warrington Gillette's full name?
215.   Does Ted ever come back to the camp?
216.   What color was Jeff's truck?
217.   Who was the last person that Jason killed?
218.   What was the first name that was shown on the Credits at the beginning of the movie?
219.   What was the last name that was shown on the Credits at the beginning of the movie?
220.   What was the first name to be shown on the Cast of Characters at the end of the movie?
221.   What was the last name to be shown on the Cast of Characters at the end of the movie?
222.   Was the Cast of Characters listed in alphabetical order?
223.   Was the Cast of Characters listed in order of appearance?
224.   Who played "The Prowler"?
225.   Who played the Jason stunt double?
226.   What did Alice ask her cat right before she got killed?

227. Where did Jason get the pickaxe he used to break the door down in the old cabin?
228. What did Ginny say when she pretended to be Jason's mother resurrected?
229. What color was Ginny's car?
230. What kind was it?
231. What color was the convertible top of Ginny's car?
232. Who owned the gas station?
233. When Jason takes the whistling teapot off the stove, you see the sleeve of his shirt, who had the same type of shirt on?
234. Who witnessed Alice's murder?
235. What did Ginny say when she found the old shack before she went inside it?
236. Who's dead body did Ginny find in the kitchen closet?
237. Who did Mark share a cabin with?
238. Who did Vicki share a cabin with?
239. Who was upstairs in the cabin that Mark was in, making out?
240. What color were the cabins?
241. How long did it take to film this movie?

Friday the 13th (Part 3) Trivia Questions

A. Matching: Match the actor or actress with the character that they portrayed.

1.	Richard Brooker	A. Chris
2.	Larry Zerner	B. Debbie
3.	Jeffrey Rogers	C. Ali
4.	Steven Susskind	D. Loco
5.	Dana Kimmell	E. Newscaster
6.	Gloria Charles	F. Jason
7.	Rachel Howard	G. Harold
8.	David Katims	H. Shelly
9.	Paul Kratka	I. Abel
10.	Cheri Maugans	J. Fox
11.	Steve Miner	K. Vera
12.	Kevin O'Brien	L. Chili
13.	Catherine Parks	M. Rick
14.	Nick Savage	N. Edna
15.	Annie Gaybis	O. Chuck
16.	Tracie Savage	P. Mrs. Sanchez
17.	Perla Walter	Q. Cashier
18.	David Wiley	R. Andy

B. Questions: Answer the following questions about the movie.

19. How many people were killed at Higgins Haven?
20. Who survived at the end of the movie?
21. Who played Jason?
22. Where did the killings happen this time?
23. What kind of vacation house was this?
24. Who finally kills Jason?
25. How is Jason killed?
26. Who was the practical joker?
27. How did he get killed?
28. Did Jason get the Hockey mask in this movie?

29. Who did Jason get the Hockey mask from?
30. Who ran into trouble with a motorcycle gang?
31. Whose car were they in?
32. Name the three members of the motorcycle gang.
33. Where were they when they got killed?
34. Who fought with Jason that luckily gave Chris a chance to grab an axe lying on the floor to destroy Jason?
35. What did Jason do to the guy that fought with him that gave Chris time to grab the axe?
36. Where did this scene take place?
37. Where did Chris hit Jason with the axe to finally destroy him?
38. Who was the last person to get killed (not including Jason)?
39. Who's dead body was thrown though a window?
40. Who was standing there when it happened?
41. Was this movie filmed in 3-D?
42. Where was Shelly when he got killed?
43. How many survived?
44. Name the people that were killed in order and how they were killed?
45. Name the bloopers in this movie.
46. Name the cut scenes?
47. Who damages the car (when Shelly and Vera had the run in with the motorcycle gang)?
48. How?
49. What was Andy doing before he got killed?
50. How many days had passed since the killings at the counselor training camp?
51. Who was the couple that owned a store, that were the first people to die?
52. Altogether, how many people were killed?
53. Where was Jason hiding out?
54. Who scared Chris when she went into the house at Higgins Haven?
55. When Chris was getting the bags out of the van, who scared her?
56. Who got to sleep in a hammock?
57. Who was Shelly's date for the weekend?
58. Who had problems with Jason before?

59. Which murder is the most memorable that Richard Brooker remembered?
60. When Chris fell out of the window, she waited for Jason to come outside, what did she use to hit him with?
61. Where did she hit him?
62. When Chris is in the van, Jason tries to strangle her, what did she do to get away?
63. How did Jason break free?
64. When she hides in the barn, where did she hide?
65. She surprises Jason, what did she do?
66. Who attacks Chris in the lake?
67. What weapon did Jason have when he followed Chris into the barn?
68. Who's dead body did Chris find in the closet?
69. What did she do that told Jason where she was hiding?
70. What did she stab Jason with when he found her in the closet?
71. Where did she stab him?
72. At the beginning of the movie, who are the two people fighting?
73. What did Ginny stab Jason with?
74. Who left the cabin?
75. Who was hurt?
76. How?
77. Describe what happened to Chris awhile ago?
78. After Rick was thrown through a window, how does Jason get into the house?
79. What weapon is he holding when he enters the house?
80. When Harold brought his pet rabbit back to it's cage, it sensed danger…why?
81. What was Edna killed with?
82. What was Harold's goldfish named?
83. Harold was trying to get his goldfish to eat, he was eating some of the fish food, he read one of the ingredients on the back of the box and then spit out the fish food, what did he read off the box?
84. When Edna caught Harold sneaking food, what was he eating?
85. How many things did Harold eat before Edna catches him?
86. What were the things that he ate?

87. At the beginning of the movie, how many dead victims were found and announced on the news?
88. Who was the only survivor announced on the news?
89. Who played the newscaster on the news?
90. At the beginning of the movie, whom did Chris and her friends think, they were being chased by?
91. What is on top of Chris's van?
92. Who played a joke on everybody after they arrived?
93. Where were Vera and Shelly when they ran into trouble with the motorcycle gang?
94. Who finds Fox dead?
95. How was she killed?
96. How was Loco killed?
97. Who finds him dead?
98. Who were the two people juggling?
99. What were they juggling?
100. What did Vera drop in the water, by accident?
101. What was the reason that she still had it?
102. Who did Chris tell about what happened to her awhile ago to?
103. When Chuck goes to the outhouse, who scares him?
104. What practical joke did Shelly play on Vera?
105. How was Andy killed?
106. Who had to go down to the basement and check the fuse box?
107. Who got electrocuted?
108. How?
109. Where did Rick tell Chris that he was going, right before he went outside and got killed?
110. How was Rick killed?
111. Name the things that Chris did to try to stop Jason.
112. Where was Chris when she found a dead body (the first time…right before Rick's)?
113. Whose dead body was it?
114. Who was not named in this movie?
115. Why did Edna scream, right before she was killed?
116. Who wrote the novel, Friday the 13th Part 3?
117. In Shelly's wallet, what was Vera looking at before she accidentally dropped it?
118. In the novel, Shelly had a last name…what was it?

119. Who was in the kitchen, when Shelly crawled back to the house (when his throat was cut)?
120. When Chris and Rick got back to the house, what was blocking the door?
121. What was burning?
122. When Chuck was being killed in the basement, what happened to the lights?
123. When Vera and Shelly were in the store, what did the cashier tell Vera?
124. What was Debbie doing before she got killed?
125. What was Vera's last name?
126. What was in the bathtub when Chris looked in it?
127. What happened to Chris, before and how did she tell Rick?
128. What game show does Edna watch on TV?
129. What was the answer to the question asked on the game show?
130. What magazine was Debbie reading in the hammock before she discovers Andy's body and what issue was it?
131. What was the original ending intended to be?
132. What does the sign above Harold and Edna's store say?
133. What did Harold have a fascination or hobby for?
134. Name the three things that show this?
135. How many hearts are decorated on the side of Chris's van?
136. How many days had it been since the killings from Part 2?
137. Where was the movie filmed?
138. Was there a blooper with the appearance of what Jason looked like from Part 2 and Part 3?
139. Who directed this movie?
140. Who produced this movie?
141. Who was the music by?
142. Who was the stunt coordinator?
143. What are the two novels that exist?
144. Who were given credit for the writing credits for the movie?
145. Who was the news reporter?
146. What news station reports this?
147. At the beginning of the movie what was Ginny Field's condition reported as?
148. Why did Chris come back to Higgins Haven?
149. At the end of the movie who does Chris dream of?

150. At the beginning of the movie who was the Chief that was mentioned?
151. At the end of the movie, did Chris start screaming in the police car and then start laughing hysterically?
152. What could you see from the window in the room that Debbie and Andy were using?
153. Was Chris staring out of the opened window at the barn, when she was showing Debbie the room?
154. When was this movie released?
155. Who distributed the movie?
156. Was the lake a man made pond?
157. How much did this film make at the box office?
158. What was the film's budget?
159. In one of the novels, Chili has a twin sister, what is her name?
160. How many movies was Richard Brooker told that there was going to be?
161. Who attacks Chris in the lake?
162. Was it a dream?
163. What is the name of the other novel?
164. Who wrote the novel, Friday the 13th (Part 3-D)?
165. Originally what was Rick's name?
166. Which novel had pictures from the movie?
167. Are the novels hard to find?
168. Where would you possibly find them?
169. Who got out of the van, when they got to Vera's house?
170. Who said, "Shelly come out and meet your date"?
171. How did Shelly reply?
172. What did Shelly call himself?
173. When Vera's mother answered the door, who says, "Hi Mrs. Sanchez, We're her to pick up Vera"?
174. What is Mrs. Sanchez's reply?
175. Who arranged for Shelly's date?
176. Who was Andy's roommate?
177. Who actually noticed the smoke first?
178. Why did Shelly, Chris, Andy, Debbie and Vera think the van was on fire?
179. When they get to the van, who was inside the van making the smoke?

180. How were they making the smoke?
181. When they arrive at Higgins Haven who runs down to the lake instead of taking their things in?
182. When they went to pick up Vera, what gag did Shelly pull?
183. Who did he pull the gag on?
184. What did Andy call Shelly?
185. What was Shelly's reply?
186. When Vera left in Rick's car, who did she almost not take with her?
187. How much was made at the box office?
188. Who starred in this movie?
189. Who co-starred?
190. Why did Dana Kimmell complain to the producers?
191. What was Ginny Field suffering from?
192. What scared Harold to make him run to the bathroom?
193. Who had no comment about the killings when reached early in the morning?
194. At the beginning of this movie was it different than how they ended Part 2?
195. Who played the TV Newscaster?
196. Did the snake scare Harold so much that he had to run to the bathroom?
197. When he rushed in, did he scare Edna?
198. What did she say to him when he rushed in?
199. Whose Summer Vacation Home was Higgin's Haven?
200. At the beginning of the movie, Chris and her friends think they are being chased; by the police, what evidence do they have to get rid of?
201. And how do they get rid of it?
202. After Chris tried to hang Jason and he did not die, what was her reply to him when he showed her his face?
203. How many names were listed at the beginning of the movie in Starring?
204. How many people co-starred at the beginning of the movie in the credits?
205. What did the sign say above Harold and Edna's store?
206. In the beginning of the movie, what was reported that Ginny was suffering from?

207. Bodies where found strewn over the how many square miles of the campground remote lake area?
208. Did the news guy say that the guy responsible for the Crystal Lake murders was still at large?
209. When Edna came out to take in the clothes, what was missing?
210. Did Edna have curlers in her hair?
211. What did Harold say that the fish food tasted like?
212. What did he say to his rabbit, he found in the lettuce?
213. What color was his rabbit?
214. Was his rabbit a big rabbit?
215. When he got to the garage did his rabbit get nervous?
216. What did Harold say to his rabbit, when his rabbit got nervous?
217. Was there a good reason his rabbit was nervous?
218. Why?
219. Where was Harold when he got killed?
220. What was Edna doing when she got killed?
221. When Chris goes to enter the house at Higgins Haven, did she find the door open a bit?
222. When did filming begin?
223. Where did filming begin?
224. How long did it take to film the movie?

Friday the 13th: The Final Chapter (Part 4)
Trivia Questions

A. Matching: Match the actors or actresses with the character they portrayed.

1.	Lisa Freeman	A. Axel
2.	Judie Aronson	B. Hitchhiker
3.	Bruce Mahler	C. Terri
4.	Alan Hayes	D. Nurse Morgan
5.	Crispin Glover	E. Mrs. Jarvis
6.	Bonnie Hellman	F. Paul
7.	Carey More	G. Jimmy
8.	Camilla More	H. Samatha
9.	Joan Freeman	I. Tommy Jarvis
10.	E. Erich Anderson	J. Doug
11.	Lawrence Monoson	K. Sara
12.	Corey Feldman	L. Ted
13.	Peter Barton	M. Trish
14.	Barbara Howard	N. Rob
15.	Kimberly Beck	O. Tina

B. Questions: Answer the following questions about the movie.

16. Who was the guy that was looking for Jason?
17. Why?
18. Who played Jason?
19. Where did Jason, escape from?
20. How many people survived?
21. Who?
22. Who finally destroyed Jason?
23. Who played him?
24. Name the cut scenes?
25. Who's tombstone was on the side of the road that the kids in the station wagon stopped next to when they argued about being lost?

26. How many people were killed?
27. Were there any off-screen kills? What were they?
28. What was the hitchhiker doing when she got killed?
29. At the beginning of the movie what was Tommy doing?
30. Name everybody that was killed in this movie and they were killed?
31. At the beginning of the movie, who was dead in the barn?
32. What were the directions to the house that the six teens rented for the weekend?
33. Who are hugging in the hospital lounge?
34. Who puts his sandwich on Jason's covered head?
35. What does Axel do to Nurse Morgan?
36. What did Nurse Morgan say she only came in the room to do?
37. What was the name of the morgue?
38. Whose hand touched Nurse Morgan's upper thigh?
39. Who breaks three bottles?
40. How does Nurse Morgan get killed?
41. Who gets killed by a hacksaw?
42. Who gets their neck broken?
43. Who goes jogging?
44. Who are having a conversation in the backseat of the station wagon?
45. Who says, "computers don't lie"?
46. What date was on the tombstone that the kids in the station wagon passed?
47. What was the name of Jarvis' dog?
48. What color is the car that the Jarvis family owns?
49. Who are the two girls talking in front of the mirror?
50. What did the hitchhiker's sign say?
51. How does the hitchhiker get murdered?
52. What does Tommy see through his bedroom window?
53. Who is Paul's girlfriend?
54. What are the names of the twins?
55. Where do they want to go?
56. Who goes back for the car?
57. Who was driving the station wagon, when they passed a tombstone?
58. Whose car breaks down on the road from Crystal Point?

59. Who threatens to submerge themselves and not come up?
60. Who got pulled into the water?
61. Who helps Tommy and Trish with the car?
62. What does Rob tell Trish and Tommy that he is hunting for?
63. What is Tommy's reply?
64. Where does Tommy take Rob?
65. What does Tommy show Rob?
66. Who gets off the couch to get a drink?
67. Whose dead body was thrown through a window?
68. Who tells Rob to return whenever possible?
69. What makes Sam angry?
70. What does Sam do?
71. Who owns a computer?
72. What two people discuss computers, again?
73. Who was mad at Paul?
74. How does Sam get killed?
75. What does Paul do when he leaves the living room?
76. Who says, "Lets go upstairs"?
77. Who holds a teddy bear?
78. Who swims to Sam in her boat?
79. How does Paul get murdered?
80. Who hears Paul scream?
81. What happens to Rob's tent?
82. What happens to Rob's rifle?
83. What did Rob show Trish?
84. What couple are in a bed when it breaks?
85. Who tries to get her sister to leave with her?
86. Who gets stabbed in the back?
87. Where is this person when they get stabbed?
88. Was Mrs. Jarvis's murder an off-screen kill?
89. When did it start storming in the movie?
90. What does Mrs. Jarvis see?
91. Who is going to lose their lollipop?
92. Whose house is empty?
93. How many kids rented the house next door to Mrs. Jarvis?
94. Where does Trish run into when she looks for Rob?
95. What does Rob do to Trish?
96. Why does Rob do what he does to Trish?

97. What is the old filmstrip about?
98. Who was singing while in the shower?
99. Who constantly swears, before he gets killed?
100. What is Jimmy looking for when he gets killed?
101. How does Jimmy get killed?
102. How old is Tommy?
103. Who was the camper?
104. What color is the flashlight?
105. What color is Tommy's hat?
106. Who is running the filmstrip?
107. How did Ted get murdered?
108. What color was the towel that Sara had around her?
109. What color is the hair dryer?
110. Who was in the shower?
111. Who did Doug think was in the bathroom?
112. What weapon did Jason use on Doug?
113. What weapon did Jason use on Sara?
114. What did Jason do outside to a wall?
115. Why did the dog whine?
116. Whose house is the dog in before he smashed through a window?
117. What happens at a thunderclap?
118. Where is the crossbow?
119. What happened to Gordan?
120. What newspaper articles does Tommy look at?
121. Where is Jason when Trish heads downstairs (next door)?
122. What did Trish find that scared her, and made her run downstairs to the basement?
123. How is Rob killed?
124. Where is Rob killed?
125. Name where Trish hit Jason trying to stop him?
126. What does Jason throw at Trish?
127. Whose television does Trish throw at Jason?
128. Who does Jason run after?
129. Where does Trish jump to?
130. What color is Trish's underwear?
131. Where does Trish hit Jason first?

132. Was Jason afraid of Trish when she was attacking him with the machete?
133. What does Trish use to knock of the mask?
134. When does Tommy stab Jason?
135. How many times does Tommy stab Jason?
136. What are the bloopers?
137. What color were Terri's shoes?
138. What color was Terri's slacks?
139. Crystal Point was actually what?
140. What did Tommy use to kill Jason?
141. When Tom Savini was called in to do the special make up effects, were they intending for this to be the last Friday the 13th movie of the series?
142. Who was the actor from Back to the Future that showed up in this movie?
143. Who did he play?
144. Where was the movie filmed?
145. What did the headline read on the newspaper the Mrs. Jarvis was reading?
146. When the kids from next door were walking to Crystal Point, who was wearing headphones?
147. Who played Rob?
148. Who played Jason?
149. What's the most memorable murder that Ted White remembered?
150. When the kids meet the twins where were they all going?
151. At the beginning of the movie why couldn't Tommy play the video game up in his room?
152. What is the name of this movie?
153. What were the names of the twins?
154. What was the name of the morgue that Jason was in?
155. What color shirt was Tommy wearing in Part 4, when he brought Rob to his room?
156. What color was the house next door to the Jarvis's?
157. When Tina was pulled out of the window, and landed on a parked car, who's car was it?
158. What kind of car was it?
159. What color was the car?

160. What color were Tina's shoes?
161. Whose dead body blocked the front door next door when Trish tried to leave?
162. What color pants was Terri wearing at the party?
163. What color pants was Tina wearing at the party?
164. What color shoes was Terri wearing at the party?
165. What was wrong with Terri's bike?
166. What did Sam say right before she gets killed?
167. Whose idea was it for Jimmy and Tina to go upstairs?
168. When Paul got killed what was he trying to do?
169. When Mrs. Jarvis gets back to an empty and dark house, what does she get to drink?
170. How many lollipops did Tommy have in his mouth when he told his sister to slow down?
171. What color was Trish's dress that she was wearing when she went into Rob's tent?
172. What color was her belt?
173. Who took a shower together?
174. What was Sara trying to do when she got killed?
175. What color eyes did Trish have?
176. What color were Rob's eyes?
177. What color are Tommy's eyes?
178. Who played Terri and Tina?
179. Who played the 2 medics?
180. Who played Jimmy?
181. Who played Tommy?
182. Who played Trish?
183. Who played Mrs. Jarvis?
184. What color was Rob's Tent?
185. At the beginning where did they find Jason?
186. Who was the first name shown on the credits at the beginning of the movie?
187. Who was the last name shown on the credits at the beginning of the movie?
188. Who was the first name listed in the Cast of Characters at the end of the movie?
189. Who was the last name listed in the Cast of Characters at the end of the movie?

190.   Were the Cast of Characters listed in alphabetical order?
191.   Were the Cast of Characters listed in order of appearance?
192.   What is Jimmy doing, before he was killed?
193.   What was Ted doing, before he was killed?
194.   What was Nurse Morgan doing before she gets killed?
195.   When was this movie filmed?
196.   Was it filmed on a Movie Ranch?
197.   Whose dead body blocked the back door?
198.   What number was on the Jarvis's license plate?
199.   Where was Sara when she was killed?
200.   What was Trish doing when she found the dead body of Doug in the bathroom?
201.   What was Trish holding when she Doug's dead body and runs down to the basement?
202.   When Jason grabbed Tommy, what did Trish hit him with to make him let go of Tommy?
203.   Where did she hit him?
204.   What color what was the Jarvis's license plate?
205.   When Tommy tried to fix the car, what did he need?
206.   Where did he look to hopefully find one?
207.   Did he find one?
208.   What did Jimmy bring down stairs and give to Ted and told him to run it through his computer?
209.   At the party, when they had a contest between Tina and Terri, who won?
210.   What kind of contest was it?
211.   What color hat was Paul wearing?
212.   What kind was it?
213.   Whose room upstairs did Timmy and Tina go in?
214.   When Terri told her sister it was time to go, what was her reply?
215.   When Terri said, "I'm going to leave without you", what was her sister's reply?
216.   What did Sara tell Doug, before she went upstairs?
217.   What was his reply?
218.   What else did she say to him?
219.   What was his reply to that?
220.   What was the last thing she said before going upstairs?

221. When Mrs. Jarvis returned and it was raining, were the lights working?
222. What did she say that she was going to do after she toweled off?
223. What was Doug singing in the shower?
224. When Sara told Doug she was going upstairs, what color was her dress that she was wearing?
225. When Sara got out of the shower, what did Doug say?
226. What was her reply?
227. Did Trish see Rob getting killed?
228. When Trish breaks the window to escape after seeing Rob getting killed what did she use to break the window?
229. Did Trish nail up the front door to the Jarvis home?
230. What color was Sara's robe that she had on?
231. What color of sweat suit was Mrs. Jarvis wearing when she returned from jogging in the rain?
232. What did Jimmy get out of the refrigerator?
233. When Trish and Tommy were hiding in Tommy's room, what did Jason use to break down the door?
234. Were Jason's fingernails long and black?
235. What did Trish yell to Tommy when she came back to the house and he was upstairs?
236. Did Jason escape from the morgue?
237. How many people went through a window thanks to Jason?
238. Who were they?
239. When Trish broke the window to escape after seeing Rob getting killed what was covering the window?
240. After Trish knocked Jason's hockey mask off, where did Tommy hit Jason?
241. What did Tommy use to hit him?
242. After Trish hit Jason in the hand, when she hit him in the chest, what did he do?
243. Which of Jason's eye was deformed?
244. Which was his good eye?
245. When Rob mentioned that Jason's body disappeared from the morgue, what was Trish's reply?
246. What was Rob's response?

247. When Jimmy and Tina were in Paul's room, what did Jimmy look around the room and say?
248. What was Tina's reply?
249. What was Jimmy's reply?
250. What did Tina say to Jimmy right before the bed breaks?
251. What was the hitchhiker doing before she was killed?
252. What did Jimmy throw at Ted?

Friday the 13th Part V: A New Beginning Trivia

A. Matching: Match the actors or actresses with the characters that they played.

1.	Dominick Brascia	A.	Roy/pseudo-Jason
2.	Corey Feldman	B.	Billy/Male Nurse
3.	Juliette Cummins	C.	Anita
4.	Ron Sloan	D.	Ethel
5.	Jerry Pavlon	E.	Matt
6.	Melaine Kinnamon	F.	Eddie
7.	Ric Mancini	G.	Tommy
8.	Bob DeSimone	H.	Robin
9.	Carol Locatell	I.	Joey
10.	Debisue Voorhees	J.	Reggie the Reckless
11.	Caskey Swaim	K.	Junior
12.	Richard Young	L.	Violet
13.	Dick Wieand	M.	Mayor Cobb
14.	Mark Venturini	N.	Vinnie
15.	Marco St. John	O.	Jake
16.	John Robert Dixon	P.	Raymond
17.	Corey Parker	Q.	George
18.	Sonny Shields	R.	Victor
19.	John Shepard	S.	Young Tommy
20.	Shavar Ross	T.	Sheriff Tucker
21.	Migel A. Nunez Jr.	U.	Deputy Dodd
22.	Tiffany Helm	V.	Neil
23.	Anthony Barrile	W.	Lana
24.	Todd Bryant	X.	Tina
25.	Jere Fields	Y.	Pam
26.	Rebecca Wood-Sharkey	Z.	Duke
27.	Vernon Washington	AA.	Nurse Yates/Receptionist
28.	Richard Lineback	BB.	Les
29.	Curtis Conaway	CC.	Pete
30.	Suzanne Bateman	DD.	Demon

A. Questions: Answer the following questions about the movie.

31.   Who did the masked man (pseudo-Jason) turn out to be at the end of the movie?
32.   Who were the two people in Tommy's dream that dug up Jason?
33.   Did one of them say why they were digging up Jason?
34.   Why were they doing it?
35.   What happens to them?
36.   Where did the killings take place?
37.   What was the name of the kid that was killed at the woodpile?
38.   How was he killed?
39.   Who killed him?
40.   Who was the third person to get killed after the woodpile murder?
41.   How was he killed?
42.   Who was the last person to get killed?
43.   How?
44.   Who was the neighbor that complained about the kids from the halfway house trespassing on her property?
45.   Who lived with her?
46.   What was the name of Reggie the Reckless's brother?
47.   What was the name of his girlfriend?
48.   Who was Reggie's grandfather?
49.   Who was in charge of the halfway house?
50.   Who was the sheriff that got chewed out by the mayor?
51.   Why?
52.   What was the sheriff's first name?
53.   Who was the mayor?
54.   Who played the mayor?
55.   Who played Joey?
56.   What relationship was Joey to Roy?
57.   In which hand was Joey carrying his half-eaten, melted candy bar?
58.   Why was Joey teased before?
59.   What did Joey say to Victor, right before; Joey is killed by Victor?
60.   Who were the two guys that were killed in Tommy's dream?

61. How did you find out, who the killer was?
62. When did you find out, who the killer was?
63. How did the pseudo-Jason die?
64. What was Joey eating before he was killed?
65. What was the color of Joey's eyes?
66. What was the color of Roy's eyes?
67. What is the number of ways that the pseudo-Jason was slowed down?
68. Who was the second person to get killed after the woodpile murder?
69. How?
70. Who played the sheriff?
71. Did he get killed?
72. Who witnessed Joey's death at the woodpile?
73. What was Pete doing right before he got killed?
74. What was the name of the halfway house that Tommy was sent to?
75. What kind of day was it when Joey got killed?
76. At the end of the movie what happened to Tommy that put him in the hospital?
77. What were the girls doing when Joey wanted to help?
78. What were the names of the two girls?
79. Who played the two girls?
80. Who was the guy chopping wood at the woodpile?
81. What was the name of the blonde-haired paramedic?
82. Where was he found dead?
83. Who finds him?
84. What did Pam attack the pseudo-Jason with?
85. Where did she cut him?
86. And at the last moment something happened, what happened?
87. How did Matt die?
88. Who found him dead?
89. Who played Matt?
90. At the beginning of the movie as Tommy arrived, what did Joey say?
91. Who did he say it to?
92. Who were the two kids that trespassed on the Hubbard's property?

93.   What was the name of the song that Violet was listening to, right before she was killed?
94.   Who was the song by?
95.   Who was the guy that stuttered a lot?
96.   How did he die?
97.   Who played him?
98.   The morning that everyone was having breakfast, who actually set too many places at the table?
99.   Who actually was the first person that told her that she set too many places?
100.   What did George say to Violet?
101.   Who gives Violet the look as if saying to her "I told you so"?
102.   What did Reggie say to Violet?
103.   What did Jake say to Violet?
104.   Who walked in and asked, "What's going on here"?
105.   Who came to the Hubbard's, wanting to earn a meal?
106.   When Reggie asked his grandpa if he could go see his brother, what did his grandpa say?
107.   What was Junior doing when the man came to the door?
108.   What was Ethel doing when the man came to her door?
109.   What was the man doing when he got killed?
110.   How did he get killed?
111.   Whose room did the pseudo-Jason put the three bodies in?
112.   Name who they were.
113.   Who finds them?
114.   At the beginning of the movie what did Tommy have in his bag?
115.   When Pam and Reggie were running down stairs who trips?
116.   Who smashed through the door?
117.   Who was the first person that the pseudo-Jason killed?
118.   How?
119.   Where was Tommy, when he was hurt by the pseudo-Jason?
120.   At the beginning of the movie, how were Neil and Les killed?
121.   Who kills them?
122.   Which murder scene were Duke and Roy at, when Roy says something?
123.   What did Sheriff Tucker tell his deputies?

124. In the scene that Roy says something, what did Sheriff Tucker first say right before Roy says something?
125. Roy says something; what did he say?
126. Who did he say it to?
127. How did the sheriff answer him?
128. One of the deputies comes over to the sheriff and says something,, what did he say?
129. Where did Tina die?
130. Who played her?
131. How did Eddie die?
132. Who played him?
133. Where was he when he died?
134. How did Robin die?
135. Where was she when she died?
136. What was Jake doing when he got killed?
137. Did Joey say he could help others there at Pine Hurst?
138. What scenes were cut from the movie?
139. After Reggie rams the pseudo-Jason, he gets wounded where?
140. How?
141. Who was the fifth person that the pseudo-Jason killed?
142. How did he get killed?
143. Who did Reggie want to go see?
144. Describe what Reggie's brother was wearing?
145. What did he give Reggie?
146. Who did Reggie introduce to his brother as his girlfriend?
147. How did Demon respond?
148. What does Demon offer Pam to eat?
149. Does she say that she's not hungry?
150. When Demon says to Reggie, "I know what you want…a beer", how did Reggie respond?
151. How did Demon answer him?
152. What was the reason that Pam told Reggie that they had to go?
153. As Reggie left what did Demon, yell to him?
154. What happened to Anita and Demon?
155. How?
156. Where did Demon die?
157. Who played Demon?
158. Who played Anita?

159. What was Junior doing when he got killed?
160. How did he get killed?
161. Who played Junior?
162. What was Ethel doing when she got killed?
163. How did she get killed?
164. When Pam went out to find everybody, she told Reggie to be somewhere by the time she got back, where was it?
165. At the beginning of the movie, when Tommy gets there, Reggie scares Tommy with something, what was it?
166. When Tommy wakes up from his dream at the beginning of the movie, where was he?
167. What were the two guys doing in Tommy's dream?
168. Who was Reggie visiting at Pine Hurst?
169. During most of the movie, Violet was wearing something; what was it?
170. In Tommy's dream, what was all over Jason when Neil and Les dug him up?
171. What weapon did Jason have in his hand when he went over to Tommy, in Tommy's dream?
172. What did it say on the van that brought Tommy to Pine Hurst?
173. On the sign at Pine Hurst, what does it say?
174. What was Joey doing before he got killed?
175. What did the Sheriff say to Matt right after Joey got killed?
176. What did Matt say about Joey's parents?
177. What color were Victor's eyes?
178. What did Reggie hit the pseudo-Jason with...when Reggie came to Pam's house?
179. Describe the scene, right before pseudo-Jason fell and was impaled on a harrow?
180. Who did Tommy keep seeing (he kept hallucinating that he saw...)?
181. Whose ankle did the pseudo-Jason grab, when he started to fall off the barn loft?
182. Who came to the rescue?
183. What did he hit the pseudo-Jason with?
184. Where?
185. As the pseudo-Jason was falling to his death, what fell off of him?

186. Please describe what a tractor harrow is?
187. What color of eyes did the pseudo-Jason have?
188. Right after Tommy was hurt by the pseudo-Jason, Tommy stabs the pseudo-Jason with what?
189. What kind of weather was it then?
190. When in the movie did it start raining?
191. Who was the last person that the pseudo-Jason killed?
192. Who were the people that were killed off screen?
193. Who's body was thrown though a window?
194. Who was standing there when it happened?
195. What was Tommy's last name?
196. What was the last name of the paramedic Roy?
197. What does Reggie say to Tommy when the police siren sounds?
198. At the beginning of the movie, what does Tommy take out of his bag?
199. At the beginning of the movie, who got Tommy to finally get out of the van?
200. Who did the police bring back to Pine Hurst?
201. Why?
202. How long had Jake and Robin been there at Pine Hurst?
203. Who made Tommy angry, when Reggie was visiting his brother?
204. After Joey's murder, when everybody was having breakfast, who made Tommy angry?
205. As Joey was getting killed, who looked out of the window?
206. How many times does Tommy actually hallucinate that he sees Jason?
207. What did Joey put his chocolate covered hands on?
208. What was the reason that Pam and Reggie got separated?
209. When Lana was still inside of the restaurant what scared her?
210. What did Joey try to share with the girls?
211. What did Joey try to give Victor?
212. Who played Tommy Jarvis?
213. In Tommy's dream at the beginning of the movie, what was the weather like?
214. In Tommy's dream at the beginning of the movie, what was Tommy carrying?

215. In Tommy's dream near the end of the movie, who did he stab?
216. What did he use to stab the person?
217. At the beginning of the movie who; did Pam introduce herself as?
218. At the beginning of the movie, who was in the picture that Tommy was looking at?
219. What was Ethel holding in her hands when the man that wanted to earn a meal came to the door?
220. What was Vinnie doing before he got killed?
221. Where did Anita die?
222. What did Duke say right before Joey's dead body was uncovered?
223. What was Joey carrying at the beginning of the movie?
224. Who was walking with him?
225. How many candy bars did Joey have?
226. What was the blonde-haired paramedic chewing?
227. Was he wearing sunglasses when he and Roy arrived at Pine Hurst because of Joey's murder?
228. Does he take them off right before they uncover Joey's dead body?
229. What was Ethel using before she grabbed her shotgun?
230. As the police car brings Eddie and Tina back to Pine Hurst, who passed the car on the left?
231. Who passed it on the right?
232. When did the killings actually start?
233. Who were the people that were not named in the movie?
234. Who was the paramedic that never talked much (not even to the other paramedics)?
235. What made paramedic Roy's mind, snap to become the pseudo-Jason?
236. What was Roy's expression as he and Duke uncovered Joey's body?
237. What did Sheriff Tucker find in Roy's wallet?
238. What did the Sheriff ask about Tommy Jarvis?
239. What did Matt say?
240. At the end of the movie, how many things did the Sheriff find in Roy's wallet?

241. Who was in the passenger's seat of the van that brought Tommy to Pine Hurst?
242. Who brought Reggie to see his brother?
243. What was the most memorable murder that Dick Wieand remembered?
244. What was the reason that Corey Feldman couldn't play Tommy Jarvis in the whole movie?
245. How did Tina die?
246. Who played Victor?
247. On the director's cut, Duke said something different than what he said on the regular rated "R" version, what did he say on both occasions?
248. Do you think that the character Joey was important to the movie? Why?
249. What did Matt say about Joey after, Joey got killed?
250. Right before Reggie tells everybody that breakfast is ready, his grandfather does something to him, what was it?
251. What was Reggie's response to what his grandfather did?
252. What did George say after Reggie says that?
253. What was Violet doing before she got killed?
254. When Jake and Robin walked in to sit down at the table for breakfast, they had a little conversation, what did they say?
255. Who called Pine Hurst "a crazy farm"?
256. Who called Pine Hurst "a nut house"?
257. Who called Pine Hurst "a loony bin"?
258. When Reggie called everyone for breakfast, who was setting the table?
259. Who was putting the napkins on the table?
260. What did Matt say to everybody when he came and sat down at the table for breakfast?
261. Was Victor, carried off by the police after he killed Joey?
262. When Billy was about to get killed who was he calling out for?
263. Where was she?
264. What color car was Vinnie and Pete's car?
265. What color was Demon's van?
266. What color was Billy's car?
267. Did Joey tell Victor that he loved being at Pine Hurst?

268. What did Reggie put on the table, for breakfast?
269. Was the axe that Victor was using to chop wood, a double bladed axe?
270. When Lana looked out of the opened driver's side door, what did she see?
271. Does Lana panic and can't get the car door open to escape?
272. Was Lana by the trunk of the car when she got killed?
273. What color was the sheet Tina was laying on?
274. Where did Tina get it?
275. Whose idea was it that Tommy should go with Reggie and Pam to see Reggie's brother?
276. Who encouraged Tommy to go?
277. Was Matt angry with Tina and Eddie for not showing up?
278. Was Reggie anxious to go and see his brother?
279. Where was Demon stabbed before he was actually killed?
280. What did Ethel say right before she got killed?
281. What smashed through the window and killed Ethel?
282. What did Lana pick up off the floor of Billy's car?
283. What room of Ethel and Junior's house do you see in the whole movie?
284. What color was Lana's waitress outfit?
285. Did Victor hate being at Pine Hurst?
286. Who died in the driver's seat of a car?
287. Who worked as a waitress at a restaurant?
288. Who worked at The Unger Institute of Mental Health?
289. When Junior was riding his bike around the outside of the house yelling to his mom, what was his mom (Ethel) doing?
290. What was Junior's dinner going to be?
291. What was Ethel putting in the pot when she was making her stew?
292. When Ethel was making her stew, she yelled to Junior outside what did she want him to do?
293. When do suspect that Matt was killed since they did not show him getting killed, you see him dead when Pam is running through the woods and runs in to him?
294. Who called Tommy "A lunatic"?
295. How did Junior know that Tommy was from Pine Hurst?

296. When you suspect that Duke was killed, since they didn't show him getting killed, but they showed him dead when Pam and Reggie find him dead in his ambulance?
297. Who played Duke?
298. What did Demon blame for running to the outhouse?
299. What color was the dress that Anita was wearing?
300. Was Reggie anxious to go and see his brother?
301. Where did Reggie go to meet his brother?
302. What color was the pick-up truck that Pam was driving?
303. Did they show Anita getting killed?
304. What did the sign; read that was next to Violet's door, on the wall?
305. When Robin is in bed what makes her turn over on her side, to find Jake's dead body lying there?
306. What did Ethel say that she would do if another one of the kids from Pine Hurst trespasses on her property again?
307. What color was Robin's robe?
308. What color was Pam's sweater that she was wearing around her shoulders?
309. When do you suppose Pam lost her sweater?
310. When did Pam and Reggie get separated?
311. Right before George's dead body was thrown through the window, who's name was Pam calling out for?
312. What was Pam yelling to Tommy when he was confronting Jason in the barn (Not knowing that it was not the real Jason)?
313. Who scared Reggie right after he found the three dead bodies in Tommy's room?
314. When Matt left, who did he tell where he was going?
315. Where was he going?
316. Who played Reggie?
317. Who played Pam?
318. Why was Tommy hallucinating about Jason?
319. Who did Pam put in charge until she got back from trying to find everybody?
320. Who played Raymond?
321. How did Reggie call everybody for breakfast?
322. What did Reggie yell?

323. What did George say after Reggie yelled for everybody to come to breakfast?
324. What did Pam say to everybody when she comes and sits down for breakfast?
325. What did Matt ask Tommy to do?
326. What was Vinnie doing right before he got killed?
327. Name the bloopers in the movies?
328. Name in order all the people who were killed and name how they were killed?
329. When Juior was riding his motorcycle around the house when his mother was fixing her stew, what did he yell at her?
330. Who killed Roy/pseudo-Jason?
331. Was Robin able to wake Reggie up, who was sleeping on the sofa?
332. What does she do?
333. When Reggie woke up, before he finds the three dead bodies in Tommy's room, what did he say?
334. How long is the movie?
335. What year was it released?
336. Who was the producer of this movie?
337. What weapon did the pseudo-Jason have in his possession when he followed Reggie and Pam into the barn?
338. How many deputies did Sheriff Tucker have?
339. How did Lana get killed?
340. How did George get killed?
341. What color was Jason's name written in?
342. Who played young Tommy (in the dream)?
343. Was Roy one of the guys that brought Tommy to Pine Hurst?
344. How old was Tommy in this movie?
345. How did Billy get killed?
346. How many years had passed from Part 4 to this movie?
347. What did Duke say to Roy, after they uncover Joey's dead body (before they leave)?
348. What weapon did the Pseudo-Jason use to kill Robin?
349. What gave you the clue that Roy was one of the guys that brought Tommy to Pine Hurst?
350. When Pam, Tommy and Reggie left to go and see Reggie's brother, what were Matt and George doing?

351. What did Anita do to annoy Demon?
352. Did the pseudo-Jason do the same thing?
353. What happened to Pam before Reggie came to her rescue?
354. What weapon did the Pseudo-Jason have when he was chasing Pam?
355. When Tommy arrived at the barn who; called out his name?
356. When was the Chainsaw fight scene filmed?
357. What weapon does the pseudo-Jason have when Pam was fighting him with a chainsaw in the barn?
358. What does "Pseudo" mean?
359. Who played Reggie the Reckless?
360. Who played Pam?
361. Who played Lana?
362. Who played Duke?
363. When Violet was dancing in her room before she was killed…you notice posters on the walls, what are they of?
364. What was Reggie's last name?
365. When Sheriff Tucker told Pam about Roy, what was Reggie doing?
366. How did the institute diagnose Tommy?
367. When Matt was looking at Tommy's records from the institution, what did he say?
368. Who was he talking to?
369. When Jake went to see Violet in her room because he needed to talk to her, what was she doing?
370. What did she say to Jake?
371. What was his reply?
372. What color was Robin's underwear?
373. What did Robin say in front of the mirror?
374. What was Robin wearing before she was killed?
375. What did Pam tell Reggie to do when he found Jake, Robin, and Violet's dead bodies in Tommy's room and she went to check?
376. How many different weapons were used in this movie to kill people with?
377. Altogether, how many people were killed in this movie, including the woodpile murder and Tommy's dreams?
378. Who survived at the end of the movie?

379. Was one of the deputies named Deputy Dodd?
380. Who played Sheriff Tucker's deputies?
381. Who played Roy/Pseudo-Jason?
382. Who played the Roy stunt double?
383. When Reggie was visiting his brother, what did it say on the sign that Tommy was standing in front of?
384. What color was it?
385. In Tommy's dream at the beginning of the movie, whose grave was Jason standing in front of?
386. At the table, when Violet set too many places…what was she yelling to Jake when Matt walked in?
387. When Duke and Roy uncovered Joey's body, who did the camera turn to when Roy turned after seeing Joey's dead body?
388. What caused Tommy to start hallucinating about Jason?
389. Did Roy say anything in the scene where he and Duke uncovered Joey's dead body?
390. Did Joey tell Victor that he never chopped wood before and it looked like fun?
391. When Reggie was visiting his brother and Tommy was standing in front of the sign; who came up and scared him?
392. Describe what Joey was wearing.
393. What color was the shirt that Victor was wearing?
394. Was Victor sweating when he was chopping wood?
395. When the sheriff brought Tina and Eddie back, what, was the first thing he said to Matt?
396. How did Matt answer the sheriff?
397. What else did the sheriff say?
398. How did Matt answer the sheriff?
399. How many kids were found over the Hubbard's woods?
400. What color was the shirt that Vinnie wore?
401. Was Vinnie wearing a leather jacket?
402. Was Pete wearing a leather jacket?
403. What color was the shirt that Pete wore?
404. Who was wearing a hat?
405. What scared Pete?
406. When Pete died in his car, what did his head hit?

407. When Tommy first hallucinated that he sees Jason, was he wearing a shirt?
408. What do you see in the trunk after Vinnie opens it?
409. What color flashing lights are on the sheriff's car?
410. What did Reggie's grandpa tell him to do when he came to see what was going on after he heard the police siren?
411. What did Reggie say to his grandpa?
412. Was the sheriff wearing a hat?
413. Were any of the deputies wearing a hat?
414. When Tina and Eddie were brought back to Pine Hurst, where was Tommy?
415. Were Roy and Duke both wearing watches?
416. Which wrist were they wearing a watch?
417. What color was the sheriff's car?
418. What number was on the side of the sheriff's car?
419. When Ethel and Junior came over to complain about the kids trespassing on their property, what did she first tell Junior?
420. What was Billy's take out order, when he went to pick up Lana?
421. What color were the croquet balls?
422. How many were not picked up?
423. How many croquet mallets were there?
424. What color were the croquet mallets?
425. What was on the ground lying near the croquet set?
426. When Demon was in the outhouse, what did it say on the wall behind him?
427. When Demon stopped singing, what did he yell?
428. When Demon dies in the outhouse, you notice somebody's name on the wall...who's was it?
429. When Robin went to bed was it raining?
430. What was Robin wearing when she went to bed?
431. What color shirt was Violet wearing before she was killed?
432. When Reggie trips (right before the pseudo-Jason busts through the door) what was Pam telling Reggie to do?
433. When Reggie gets separated from Pam, when he is running does he fall?
434. What color shirt was Pam wearing?
435. What kind of pants was Pam wearing?

436. Right before the chainsaw fight, where was Pam hiding?
437. What was above the door of where Pam was hiding?
438. What did the sheriff say to Ethel?
439. How did she respond?
440. What did the sheriff say; before, he was interrupted off by Ethel?
441. What did Ethel say when she interrupted the sheriff?
442. Who interrupted Ethel when she was talking to the sheriff?
443. What did Junior say to her?
444. How did she respond to Junior's remark?
445. Was there any laughing after Ethel's respond to Junior's remark?
446. When Joey walked out the door, what do you see lying in the porch swing?
447. What else doe Joey pass as he was going over to the girls?
448. After Reggie and Pam ran out of the house into the woods, does she say anything to Reggie?
449. After Joey walks out the front door, does he close it?
450. When Reggie and Pam ran out of the house into the woods, what does she say to Reggie?
451. Who sees the Paramedic's vehicle?
452. Who yells, "Please help us"?
453. Who opens the door of the Paramedic's vehicle?
454. When Pam screams at the sight of Duke's dead body, how does the Pseudo-Jason show up?
455. Who sees him first?
456. When Pam was fighting Pseudo-Jason in the barn was Reggie cheering her on?
457. What color was the barn?
458. What color was the door of the barn?
459. What year was this movie released?
460. Who's room did the Pseudo-Jason put the three bodies in?
461. Name who they are.
462. Who finds them?
463. What was the reason that Corey Feldman couldn't play Tommy Jarvis in the whole movie?
464. What was the name of the song that Violet was listening to and dancing to, before she got killed?

465. Who was it by?
466. Does she get killed at the end of the song?
467. When does Violet get killed?
468. When you see the door to her room open, what do you see?
469. When Violet was dancing, did she hear a noise that made her stop dancing for a minute?
470. After Tommy's nightmare, whom does he see at the foot of his bed?
471. When Pam went to Tommy's room at the hospital, does she hear a crash?
472. What happened?
473. Was it still storming and raining at the end of the movie?
474. Who played the second deputy?
475. Who played the third deputy?
476. Who played Nurse Yates/Receptionist?
477. Were the Cast of Characters listed in alphabetical order at the end of the movie?
478. Who was listed first?
479. Who was listed last?
480. When the kids were brought back to Pine Hurst at the beginning of the movie, was Sheriff Tucker smoking a cigar?
481. Which hand was he holding it in?
482. What was Reggie wearing at the beginning of the movie, when Tina and Eddie were brought back to Pine Hurst?
483. When do you notice him wearing something different?
484. Who asked whom if they were scared of the dark?
485. Who asked whom if they were creeped out about the murders at the nut house?
486. How did he reply?
487. What was Junior using to eat his chicken stew?
488. What kind of bowl was he eating out of?
489. Name some of the kinds of clothes that the girl's were hanging out to dry as Joey walks up to them?
490. What color shirt was Victor wearing?
491. What was Tommy wearing in the dream at the beginning of the movie?
492. Who were looking for Jason's grave in Tommy's dream?

493. At the beginning of the movie, after Tommy wakes up from his dream, what is Billy/Male Nurse looking at?
494. When Tommy arrives at Pine Hurst, what color shirt is he wearing?
495. In Tommy's room was there a bulletin board?
496. Was there anything on it?
497. What was on it?
498. What was Robin wearing around her shoulders in the first part of the movie?
499. What color was it?
500. When Joey goes up to Vic and says, "Hi", what does Vic say to him?
501. What is Joey's reply?
502. When Joey said, "Don't tell the girls", Violet made a comment what was it?
503. What color dress was Demon's girlfriend wearing?
504. Was Demon wearing silver chains around his neck?
505. What color shirt was Jake wearing?
506. What color shirt was Matt wearing?
507. What color shirt was Raymond wearing?
508. What color shirt was Reggie wearing at breakfast?
509. What color shirt was Eddie wearing when he played the joke that made Tommy angry?
510. What color shirt was Violet wearing when she was killed?
511. Who was lying on a sheet completely naked when she gets killed?
512. Where did Eddie go to wash up?
513. At first, did Eddie think she was sleeping?
514. When Junior scared Tommy when Reggie was visiting his brother, how did Junior know that Tommy was from Pine Hurst?
515. How many people survived at the end of this movie?
516. Name who they are.
517. Who brought Tommy to Pine Hurst?
518. What weapon did the pseudo-Jason use the most to kill with in this movie?
519. What color shirt was Junior wearing?
520. What kind of candy bar was Joey eating?

521. Who directed this movie?
522. Why wasn't Jason in this movie?
523. When Reggie was running with Pam near the end of the movie, what was he wearing?
524. What did Reggie do right before the Pseudo-Jason burst through the door?
525. What was the difference between the Pseudo-Jason's hockey mask and the real Jason Voorhees?
526. What color shirt was George wearing?
527. What color was the paramedic's vehicle?
528. Who was the first name shown on the credits at the beginning of the movie?
529. How many scenes was Duke in?
530. When Sheriff Tucker told Mayor Cobb, he knew who was responsible for the murders…who was it?
531. What was Mayor Cobb's response to what Sheriff Tucker said?
532. How many scenes, was Roy in (as Roy the paramedic not Pseudo-Jason)?
533. What did Mayor Cobb say to Sheriff Tucker before he left?
534. After Mayor Cobb left, what did Sheriff Tucker do?
535. Where were Mayor Cobb and Sheriff Tucker when Mayor Cobb was chewing Sheriff Tucker out?
536. After Joey gets killed what does Matt say to Sheriff Tucker about Joey's dad?
537. How many scenes, was Mayor Cobb in?
538. What made Tommy's nightmares haunt him once more?
539. How many scenes, was Matt in?
540. When did filming start?
541. Who was the last name to be shown on the credits at the beginning of the movie?
542. How long did Raymond say it has been since he's last eaten?
543. How many scenes, was Neil in?
544. How many scenes, was Les in?
545. How many scenes, was Joey in?
546. How many scenes, was Victor in?
547. What did Sheriff Tucker say after Mayor Cobb said, "His body was cremated, he's nothing but a hand full of ash"?

548. What color was Reggie's sweat suit that he was wearing?
549. What color was the road flare that Vinnie was killed with?
550. How many scenes, was Corey Feldman in?
551. How many scenes, was Raymond in?
552. How many scenes, was George in?
553. What color was the trailer park sign?
554. When Roy/Pseudo-Jason was killed, who was present at the barn?
555. What color was the house that Joey came out of?
556. What color was the door that Joey shut?
557. When offered his candy bar to the girls what did Violet say?
558. When Joey left the girls, what did he say to them?
559. How did they respond?
560. What was the name of the movie that Robin and Jake where watching?
561. What did Jake say before Robin laughs (before he gets mad)?
562. When the van pulls up at Pine Hurst at the beginning of the movie and George walks by, what was he carrying over his shoulder?

Friday the 13th (Part 6) Jason Lives Trivia Questions

A. Matching: Match the actors and actresses with the characters they portrayed.

1.	C.J. Graham	A. Allen
2.	Thom Matthews	B. Darren
3.	Jennifer Cooke	C. Lizabeth
4.	Ron Palillo	D. Burt
5.	Roger Rose	E. Stan
6.	Tony Goldwyn	F. Jason Voorhees
7.	Nancy McLoughlin	G. Katie
8.	Wallace Merck	H. Larry
9.	Matthew Faison	I. Martin
10.	Ann Ryerson	J. Steven
11.	Alan Blumenfeld	K. Megan
12.	Bob Larkin	L. Annette
13.	Cynthia Kania	M. Nikki
14.	Darcy Demoss	N. Cort
15.	Whitney Rydbeck	O. Sissy
16.	Tom Fridley	P. Paula
17.	Renee Jones	Q. Roy
18.	Michael Nomand	R. Officer Pappas
19.	Kerry Noonan	S. Sheriff Garris
20.	David Kagen	T. Deputy Rick Cologne
21.	Michael Swan	U. Officer Thorton
22.	Vincent Guastaferro	V. Tommy

B. Questions: Answer the following questions about the movie.

23. Who was Tommy's friend that was there at Jason's grave with Tommy?
24. What happened to Tommy's friend?
25. How?
26. How did Martin die?
27. Who was Martin?

57

28.   At the beginning of the movie what did Tommy do?

29.   How does Jason come back to life?

30.   The name of Crystal Lake was changed to what?

31.   Why was the name changed?

32.   Who was responsible for sending Jason to his watery grave?

33.   And where was the watery grave?

34.   Who played Jason?

35.   Who was responsible for bringing Jason back to life?

36.   What were Tommy and his friend going to do to Jason?

37.   What vicinity is Jason's grave in the cemetery?

38.   When was Jason supposedly buried?

39.   What was Jason covered with when Tommy opened the coffin?

40.   When does it start raining?

41.   What does Tommy say to Jason's corpse?

42.   What does Tommy throw in the casket?

43.   What does Allen say to Tommy, when Tommy tried to pull out the metal pole?

44.   What happens to Allen?

45.   What does Tommy do when Jason goes after him?

46.   Where does Tommy go to get help?

47.   Does the Sheriff believe Tommy's story?

48.   Who drives through the fog when Jason is on the prowl?

49.   How does Darren get killed?

50.   How does Lizabeth get killed?

51.   What does she try to give Jason?

52.   What is the name of the sheriff's daughter?

53.   Does the sheriff go to Crystal Lake?

54.   What supplies are brought to Camp Crystal Lake?

55.   What was the date?

56.   Who says she'd rather deal with old Jason than the kids?

57.   What does Katie do to the men?

58.   How upset is Burt?

59.   What is Burt murdered with?

60.   Is the sheriff sure of himself?

61.   Who witnesses three decapitations?

62.   Where does Tommy lead the Sheriff, to?

63.   What was the name of the caretaker of the cemetery?

64. Did Martin cover up Jason's grave?
65. Who is Rick?
66. Does Tommy heed Sheriff Garris's orders?
67. Where is Martin when he is killed?
68. What two people are impaled with Jason's machete?
69. What little girl had a nightmare about a monster?
70. Who was the monster?
71. Who is Horace?
72. Who inspects the electrical cord?
73. Who is in the motor home?
74. What is the song playing in the motor home?
75. Who is the song by?
76. Who is the young woman that gets killed?
77. Where does she get killed?
78. How does Cort die?
79. What happens to the motor home?
80. What color was the phone in the sheriff's office?
81. What were the books about that Tommy had bought?
82. What was the most memorable murder that CJ Graham remembered?
83. Whose murder was that?
84. Who calls Megan at the sheriff's office?
85. Where is Megan going to meet Tommy?
86. How long will this take for them to meet?
87. Whose body was found dismembered?
88. What's the first thing that Jason does at the camp?
89. Whose wearing the number "37" Tee-shirt?
90. What does the back of the tee-shirt say?
91. Who is the first to get murdered at the camp?
92. Who does the sheriff think is responsible for the murders?
93. What kind of car does Megan have?
94. What theme song is playing?
95. Whose body does Jason carry past the cabin window?
96. Who chases Megan and Tommy in her car?
97. Who says, "It's the end of the line"?
98. What does Sheriff Garris call Tommy?
99. Who says, "Okay, Flash, back into the cage"?
100. Who goes outside to investigate night sounds?

101. Who gets killed and then thrown out a window?
102. Who crushes a bug on their newspaper?
103. What does Megan take from Rick?
104. What happens to Rick?
105. What is Tommy's plan to finally destroy Jason?
106. How does Jason get scared away from Nancy?
107. Who is walking on the dock with a flashlight?
108. How does he get killed?
109. Who was in the bushes in front of Officer Pappas?
110. Where is Nancy?
111. What order did Sheriff Garris' give to the kids?
112. Where does Sheriff find Jason?
113. What happens when Sheriff Garris' shotgun runs out of ammo?
114. What does Tommy find in the boat?
115. What is in Tommy's bag?
116. What does Tommy move?
117. What was in the sheriff's car?
118. At first, did the Sheriff think that Tommy was behind the killings?
119. What happened to Sheriff Garris?
120. What names does Tommy call Jason?
121. Why does Tommy call Jason these names?
122. Does it work?
123. What does Tommy pour in the water?
124. Does Tommy die when he is under the water?
125. What does Megan do when she is in the water?
126. What broke Jason's neck?
127. What does Tommy say after Jason, drowns?
128. Is Jason dead?
129. Name the bloopers in this movie.
130. Name everybody that got killed and how they were killed.
131. Were there any cut scenes?
132. What were they?
133. Who broke the boat in half that Tommy was in?
134. What did Tommy put around Jason's neck?
135. Who wanted to see that Jason got to his final "resting place"?
136. Was there a full moon at the beginning of the movie?

137. What color is Megan's car?
138. What color was Tommy's pick-up truck?
139. At the beginning of the movie, who was driving Tommy's pickup truck?
140. At the beginning of the movie, as soon as lightning hits Jason, what happened?
141. How many people survived?
142. How many people were killed?
143. Who drowns Tommy?
144. Who revives him?
145. Did Megan's plan work to get Tommy out of the jail cell?
146. Who was driving the motor home while Nikki was getting killed?
147. Who did the motor home belong to?
148. Who said, "Unless you want to look like this cord, let's make this place a memory"?
149. What did Allen hit Jason with?
150. Where did he hit him?
151. How did Tommy open Jason's coffin?
152. After Tommy stabs Jason with the metal pole, what did Allen say?
153. Who does Jason look at of the kids?
154. Does the sheriff notice that one little girl was not in her bed?
155. Who was not in her bed?
156. Whose dead body does the Sheriff find before he finds Jason?
157. After Tommy pours the gasoline in the water around the boat in the lake, what does he do next?
158. Whose murder was the most memorable that CJ Graham remembered?
159. Where was the movie filmed?
160. Who directed this movie?
161. Who was the producer of this movie?
162. Who was the music by?
163. What year was the movie released?
164. How long is the movie?
165. Who was the stunt coordinator?
166. Name the two songs that were in the movie by Alice Cooper?

167. When they were filming the final scenes in the lake in Georgia, what was the problem with the lake?
168. Who did the Special Make-up effects?
169. What was the date that this movie was released?
170. What was the name of the 12 year old boy that said, "I think we're dead meat, real dead meat"?
171. Who was he talking to?
172. How did he respond to Tyen?
173. How did the sheriff get killed?
174. Did the director's wife have a part in this movie?
175. What was her name?
176. Who did she play?
177. How did her character get killed?
178. Who distributed this movie?
179. How much money was made at the box office?
180. Because of the leeches in the lake where they were filming the final scenes; were the close up shots done later on a leechless sound stage?
181. Who starred in the movie?
182. Right before the kids arrived at the camp, who spoke of the legend?
183. Who played Sissy?
184. In the article in Entertainment Weekly called "Who Were Those Masked Men", what did CJ Graham say about playing Jason?
185. Who was in this movie that played in the TV show, "Welcome Back Kotter"?
186. What character did he play in this movie?
187. How did his character get killed?
188. Who played Sissy?
189. Did Tommy's plan to put Jason in his final resting place…at the bottom of Crystal Lake, work?
190. What did Tommy call his friend?
191. Did Tommy's friend tell him that he really didn't like what they were doing at the cemetery?
192. When Tommy was trying to remove the metal pole after lightning struck it, did Hawes suggest that he and Tommy leave?

193. Did Tommy take his friend's advice?
194. Who hollered when Jason was trying to pull Tommy into his grave?
195. Did Tommy call out to his friend as Jason killed him?
196. Did Tommy make a dramatic entrance in the sheriff's office?
197. Did Tommy, almost get shot by the sheriff as he made his dramatic entrance?
198. Who were Darren and Lizabeth?
199. What did the sheriff say that his deputy was dying to use?
200. What did one kid say to another kid, when Cort was talking about Indian Markers?
201. What did Steven give Annette?
202. Why was CJ Graham the second person picked for the role of Jason?
203. Was Megan the Sheriff's daughter?
204. Was Megan's mom dead?
205. Did Megan like Tommy?
206. Who played Tommy?
207. Who played Megan?
208. What cemetery was Jason buried in?
209. What does it say on the back of the movie box?
210. At the end of the movie, when they show a close up of Jason's eye, does he open it?
211. What color are Jason's eyes?
212. In the novel, it described Jason's dad Elias Voorhees...tell how it described him.
213. What was Jason's first weapon in Part 6?
214. When did filming begin?

Friday the 13th (Part 7): The New Blood
Trivia Questions

A. Matching: Match the actors and actresses with the character they portrayed.

1.	Lar Park Lincoln	A. Jane
2.	Terry Kiser	B. Michael
3.	Susan Blu	C. Dan
4.	Kevin Blair	D. Judy
5.	Kane Hodder	E. Russell
6.	William Butler	F. Sandra
7.	Larry Cox	G. Maddy
8.	Michael Schroeder	H. Tina
9.	Diana Barrows	I. Nick
10.	Debora Kessler	J. Ben
11.	Heidi Kozak	K. Jason Voorhees
12.	Craig Thomas	M. David
14.	Diana Almeida	N. Eddie
15.	Jeff Bennett	O. Robin
16.	Jon Renfield	P. Melissa
17.	Susan Jennifer Sullivan	Q. Dr. Crews
18.	Jennifer Banko	R. Amanda Shepherd
19.	Staci Greason	S. Tina's dad (John Shepherd)
20.	John Otrin	T. Young Tina

B. Questions: Answer the following questions about the movie.

21. Who played Jason?
22. How was Jason released from his watery grave?
23. How is Jason finally destroyed?
24. By who?
25. What happened to Tina's dad?
26. What was the month and day that the accident for Tina's dad happened?
27. Who did Tina meet next door that she liked?

28. How did Dr. Crews get killed?
29. Who was the last person to get killed?
30. How many people survived?
31. What is the name of Tina's doctor that was there, to help her?
32. Why did Dr. Crews want Tina to focus on the matchbook?
33. At the beginning of the movie, what is said?
34. What did Tina try to do?
35. Instead who is released from his watery grave in Crystal Lake?
36. Who did Tina see that came out of the lake?
37. What did she do after seeing him?
38. What did Tina find in her back porch?
39. Who was the first person that Jason killed?
40. How did Jason kill him?
41. How did his girlfriend get killed?
42. What was her name?
43. What relationship was Nick to Michael?
44. Who was the woman in a yellow sleeping bag that got killed?
45. How?
46. How did her boyfriend Dan get killed?
47. What weapon was Dan using when he got killed?
48. Who were the kids next door throwing a party for?
49. How did Tina's mom get killed?
50. What was her name?
51. What did Melissa do to upset Tina?
52. What did Tina do to her?
53. How did Russell get killed?
54. How did Sandra get killed?
55. Name the bloopers.
56. Name the cut scenes.
57. Name in order everybody that was killed and how.
58. Name everything that Tina does to Jason, when she was trying to destroy him?
59. What is it called that Tina has?
60. When Dr. Crews walked in the woods, whose dead body does he find?
61. What weapon does he find?
62. What was all over it?

63. What did Robin find in a closet?
64. Why did Dr. Crews have blood all over him?
65. Who survived?
66. How many were killed?
67. What happened to the house?
68. What did Tina see that made her crash into a tree?
69. What time of day was it when she crashed into a tree?
70. Which side of Jason's hockey mask was broken?
71. What was Jason doing, when Tina broke the hockey mask that Jason was wearing in two?
72. What color eyes did Jason have?
73. What was around Jason's neck?
74. What does the police find at the end of the movie?
75. Who gets taken away by an ambulance?
76. Who was with Tina's mom when she got killed?
77. When Tina sees Jason's face after breaking the hockey mask in two pieces, what did she do?
78. After the house blows up, was Jason dead?
79. How old was Tina when her dad had his fatal accident?
80. What caused the house to blow up?
81. What were the newspaper articles about, that Tina finds in the desk?
82. What year was this movie made?
83. How long is this movie?
84. How many different weapons did Jason use to kill his victims with?
85. After Tina looked at the newspaper articles, what did she do?
86. Who played Tina?
87. Who played Nick?
88. Who played Tina's mom?
89. What was scary about Jason in this movie?
90. Who played Dr. Crews?
91. When Jason was released from his watery grave do you see his spine?
92. Right before Tina's dad's accident what did he do?
93. Right before Tina's dad had his accident where is Tina?
94. What did she say to him?
95. Did Tina believe that it was her fault for her father's death?

96. At the beginning of the movie in the flash back does Jason's tombstone explode into pieces?
97. Was Jason scary in this movie?
98. What is the most memorable murder that Kane Hodder remembers?
99. Whose murder was it?
100. Why were Michael and Jane stranded?
101. How many miles were they from Camp Crystal Lake?
102. At the beginning of the movie (in the flashback) what happened to Jason's tombstone when he was struck by lightning?
103. What time of day was it when Tina's dad got killed?
104. What was the date that her father got killed?
105. Who is in the first scene of the beginning of the movie?
106. What kind of character was Dr. Crews?
107. Who volunteers to help Tina pick up her personals?
108. Who did Tina think about when she moved the matchbook?
109. When does Tina's mental powers work best?
110. What time of day does Tina revive Jason by accident?
111. What was Jane carrying?
112. What does Michael see that makes him run?
113. Does Michael die right away?
114. Who ran into a lamp?
115. Who says, "What a stupid place to put a lamp"?
116. Who is reluctant to get the wood?
117. What made Dan turn his head around?
118. What does Judy say right before she gets killed?
119. Was there a blooper about Judy's murder?
120. Who was spying on Nick and Tina?
121. What were Sandra and Russell doing before they were killed?
122. Who covered himself with party streamers?
123. What does Amanda find in Dr. Crew's office?
124. What color is the car that Amanda has?
125. How does David get killed?
126. What does David call out to?
127. How does Maddy get killed?
128. Where does Maddy get killed?
129. What is the name of the weapon that Jason used on Maddy?

130. Why does Ben leave the van?
131. Who did Ben think was outside?
132. What were Robin and David doing when the lights went out?
133. What did David tell Robin that he had to go?
134. Why?
135. What colors were the pillowcases?
136. What colors were the party balloons?
137. What color was David's underwear?
138. What was all over the kitchen floor, when David went to the refrigerator?
139. When David is going to the refrigerator and he's in the kitchen and there is no electricity, when lightning flashes do you see Jason over in the corner of the room?
140. What was David doing when he got killed?
141. Where did Tina and Nick get the gun?
142. What happened in there?
143. What gift did Eddie unwrap?
144. What color shirt does Robin put on?
145. Whose room does Robin go into?
146. Who picks up a cat?
147. What color cat was it?
148. Did Jason kill the cat?
149. What weapon did Jason use on Ben?
150. Who does Nick draw on?
151. Does Tina look for her mother?
152. What tool does Jason use to kill Dr. Crews?
153. Where does Tina find Kate?
154. When Tina finds Kate, was she dead?
155. What two color balloons are by the door when Tina runs into the house?
156. Where is Melissa going when she leaves Tina and Nick?
157. Did Maddy scream right as Jason killed her?
158. What does Jason pull off of Tina?
159. Is Jason really dead, at the end of this movie?
160. What did Maddy lose in the woods?
161. How did Melissa die?
162. Who told Maddy, "You need a little touch up work"?
163. Who does Maddy, go out in the woods looking for?

164. What is the first weapon used to kill the first two people?
165. Who gave Melissa her pearl necklace?
166. What was the reason she was given it?
167. Who was beheaded with a machete?
168. Who was thrown through a window?
169. How many miles from Crystal Lake were Tina and her mom, when Tina wakes up from her dream?
170. Who did Tina claimed that she saw getting killed by Jason with a metal spike?
171. Did Maddy find her missing earring?
172. What color were Maddy's earrings?
173. Whose birthday was it?
174. Who accidentally told Michael about the surprise party for him?
175. Who drinks something and strangles on it?
176. Is Kane Hodder a stuntman?
177. Where was this movie filmed?
178. Who directed this movie?
179. Who was the producer of this movie?
180. Whose car did Tina pass on the road, before she crashes into a tree?
181. Who was the stunt coordinator?
182. Why didn't Michael show up for the party?
183. Where did Nick say he grew up?
184. Did Nick say he hung around a real bad crowd and that now he was going to night school?
185. What catch phrase did Cousin Michael, use?
186. When was this movie released?
187. What was the film's budget?
188. How much money was made at the box office?
189. Who distributed this movie?
190. How many scripts were there supposedly before the director chose one?
191. Did Maddy scream right as Jason killed her?
192. Who was the character that Lar Park Lincoln played?
193. Whose bedroom door did Robin try to open but it was locked?
194. Who did Nick try to call on the phone?
195. Who starred in this movie?

196. What did Lar Park Lincoln say that she once touched and then went crazy?
197. When Tina and her mom arrive, who were laying out getting some sun?
198. Who says, "There goes the neighborhood"?
199. Who fussed at everybody for eating his uncle's food?
200. Who did Nick say he was going to go and look for in the woods?
201. Was this Kane Hodder's first movie role of playing Jason?
202. What color dress did Maddy wear?
203. What color was her belt and shoes?
204. Did her necklace match her earrings?
205. Who did David think was behind him before he was killed?
206. How long did this movie to take to film?
207. How many miles were Michael and Jane from Crystal Lake, by the sign they pass?
208. What did David notice all over the floor when he was at the refrigerator?
209. What was his response to it?
210. Who put the mud all over the floor?
211. How tall is Jason Voorhees?
212. How long does it take for Kane Hodder to be made up as Jason?

Friday the 13th (Part 8): Jason Takes Manhattan Trivia Questions

A. Matching: Match the actor or actress with the character they portrayed.

1.	Alex Diakun	A.	Rennie
2.	Kane Hodder	B.	Sean Robertson
3.	David Longworth	C.	Jim
4.	Peter Mark Richman	D.	Suzie Donaldson
5.	Michael Benyaer	E.	Cop
6.	V.C. Dupree	F.	JJ
7.	Roger Barnes	G.	Tamara
8.	Barbara Bingham	H.	Jason Voorhees
9.	Sam Sarkar	I.	Wayne
10.	Tod Shaffer	J.	Deck Hand
11.	Tiffany Paulsen	K.	Jim Carlson
12.	Saffron Henderson	L.	Admiral Robertson
13.	Fred Henderson	M.	Eva
14.	Warren Munson	N.	Miles
15.	Kelly Hu	O.	Julius
16.	Gordon Currie	P.	Gang Banger #1
17.	Sharlene Martin	Q.	Collen Van Deusen
18.	Martin Cummins	R.	Gang Banger #2
19.	Ace	S.	Charles McCullough
20.	Scott Reeves	T.	Young Jason
21.	Jensen Daggett	U.	Sanitation Worker
22.	Vinnie Capone	V.	Young Rennie
23.	Timothy Burr Mirkovich	W.	Toby
24.	Amber Pawlick	X.	New York Waitress
25.	Peggy Hedden	Y.	Street Urchin

B. Questions: Answer the following questions about the movie.

26. Where did the first part of the movie take place?
27. Where did the last part of the movie take place?

28.   Who was the last person to get killed?
29.   Who played Jason?
30.   What kind of pet does Rennie have?
31.   Was the Statue of Liberty lit at the beginning of the movie?
32.   Where were the first two people killed?
33.   What were their names?
34.   What brings Jason back to life?
35.   Was the legend Jim spoke of true?
36.   What prank did Jim play on Suzie?
37.   Where is Suzie when she is murdered?
38.   How is Suzie murdered?
39.   How many years had it been since Jason drowned?
40.   Who is the lady that joins Rennie on the graduation trip?
41.   What does the lady give Rennie as a present?
42.   What does Renee stab Jason with?
43.   What is the name of the high school?
44.   When will the class graduate?
45.   How does Jason come aboard the cruise ship?
46.   Who is Sean Robertson's father?
47.   Name the bloopers.
48.   What does Admiral Robertson give his son?
49.   Who exclaimed that the voyage was doomed?
50.   What was the name of the cruise ship?
51.   What did Sean give Rennie?
52.   Who films J.J. playing the electric guitar?
53.   Who carries around the video camrecorder?
54.   Who gets killed in the power room?
55.   When does it start storming?
56.   How does the white boxer get killed?
57.   How does Tamara get back at Rennie?
58.   Who jumps in after Rennie?
59.   Tamara offers whom a glass of champagne?
60.   How does Tamara get killed?
61.   How does Jim Carlson get killed?
62.   What happens to Admiral Robertson?
63.   How?
64.   Did Sean's father make Sean Captain of the ship?
65.   Who scares Rennie when she was letting down the anchors?

66.   Who finds Tamara dead?
67.   How does Eva get killed?
68.   Who did Wayne accidentally shoot?
69.   Who are the three boys who plan to destroy Jason?
70.   Who takes the rifle and becomes the leader?
71.   What room does Wayne investigate?
72.   What weapon does Wayne carry?
73.   How is Wayne killed?
74.   What does Wayne stumble over?
75.   What causes the engine room to catch on fire?
76.   Why couldn't Wayne see?
77.   What does Jason hit?
78.   Who tries to rationalize the Legend of Jason?
79.   Who got impaled on a deck post?
80.   Who does Jason grab and throw overboard?
81.   Who did Rennie stab?
82.   What room explodes?
83.   Where were seven anonymous students waiting?
84.   Who runs scared with the kitchen knife?
85.   What room floods the lower deck?
86.   Who lowers the lifeboat?
87.   Who is Collen Van Deusen?
88.   How does the deck hand die?
89.   What does the lightning strike?
90.   As everyone evacuates the ship, who looks down on them?
91.   Who was in the stormy water?
92.   Can Jason swim?
93.   How many survivors are in the lifeboat going to Manhattan?
94.   How many anonymous students were left on the burning ship to die?
95.   Who realizes they are in Manhattan?
96.   How does he know this?
97.   Who were rowing the lifeboat?
98.   What shape is the lifeboat?
99.   Who falls asleep?
100. What song does Julius sing?
101. What do the muggers do?
102. Who swims to New York?

103. Who do the muggers kidnap?
104. Who do the muggers shoot at?
105. Who tries to follow the muggers?
106. What do the muggers nickname Rennie?
107. How do the muggers get killed?
108. Who kills them?
109. Why does Rennie live?
110. Who does Julius try to call?
111. What does Julius say to Jason right before he is killed?
112. How is Julius killed?
113. What falls into the dumpster from the top of the building?
114. Who tells Sean that Jason is in New York?
115. Who gets killed off-screen?
116. Who runs Jason over?
117. Why did the police car explode?
118. Who makes it out of the car?
119. Who didn't make it out of the car?
120. What memory does Rennie have after the car crash?
121. Does Jason die after he was run over?
122. Who gets punched?
123. Who gets drowned in a barrel of sewage?
124. Who gets thrown out of the window?
125. Who kiss?
126. Who goes into the subway car?
127. What does Sean pull on the subway?
128. Who gets electrocuted on the subway tracks?
129. Who looks back and sees Jason?
130. What does Jason kick?
131. In response to what Jason does what goes the gang members say?
132. What does Jason do?
133. Did the gang members run away? What did they say as they ran away?
134. What was the name of the coast guard cutter that was radioed for help?
135. What does Jason do to the diner worker?
136. When Rennie told the restaurant waitress that a maniac was trying to kill them, what did the waitress say to them?

137. What does the sewer flood over with at night?
138. What time does this happen?
139. What happened to the sanitation worker?
140. What did Rennie say to Jason to get him to follow her?
141. What did Rennie throw at Jason?
142. Did lightning hit the Statue of Liberty?
143. How high is the Statue of Liberty?
144. Who shows up when Sean and Rennie kiss and hug at the end of the movie?
145. Who played young Jason?
146. What was the name of Rennie's dog?
147. On the credits at the end of the movie, what are the two muggers called?
148. Name the cut scenes.
149. Name everybody and how they were killed.
150. Who's decapitated head did they find in the police car?
151. Who does Jason get the hockey mask from this time?
152. What was the name of the small boat that the first people were killed by Jason?
153. Who were caught using drugs?
154. Who caught them?
155. Where was this movie filmed?
156. Who directed this movie?
157. At the end of the movie, after the toxic waste disappeared what was left of Jason?
158. Who was the producer of this movie?
159. How many people were killed?
160. How many people survived?
161. Who survived?
162. At the end of the movie, how was Jason destroyed?
163. How long is this movie?
164. What year was it released?
165. How did Rennie say her parents died?
166. Was the deck hand "a prophet of doom"?
167. Name the other people from the other Fridays that were also considered, "prophets of doom".
168. Who was the music by?
169. Who distributed this movie?

170. How much money was made at the box office?
171. Did they sell the movie rights after this movie?
172. Who did they sell the movie rights to?
173. What can Kane Hodder do at will?
174. Was this the first Friday the 13th that Kane Hodder was in?
175. How long did it take to film?
176. How did Kane Hodder prepare for the scene where Jason throws up?
177. Was this the last Friday the 13th movie Kane Hodder was in?

Jason Goes to Hell: The Final Friday
Trivia Questions (Part 9)

A. Matching: Match the actors or actresses with the character they portrayed.

1.	Kane Hodder	A.	Coroner
2.	Richard Gant	B.	Coroner's Assistant
3.	Dean Lorey	C.	FBI Agent #1
4.	Michelle Clunie	D.	FBI Agent # 2
5.	Michael Silver	E.	Alexis
6.	Madeon Curtis	F.	Deborah
7.	Andrew Bloch	G.	Lou/Luke, the boy camper
8.	Erin Gray	H.	Edna
9.	Kipp Marcus	I.	Josh
10.	Tony Ervolina	J.	Diana
11.	Kathryn Atwood	K.	Robert Campbell
12.	Diana Georger	L.	Officer Mark
13.	Mark Thompson	M.	Officer Ryan
14.	Adam Cranner	N.	Jason Voorhees
15.	Brain Phelps	O.	Ward
16.	Kane Hodder	P.	Shelby
17.	Leslie Jordan	Q.	Officer Brian
18.	Jason D. LeMay	R.	Vicki
19.	Rusty Schwimmer	S.	Randy
20.	Allison Smith	T.	Steven Freeman
21.	Steven Culp	U.	Jessica Kimble
22.	Steven Williams	V.	Joey B.
23.	Kari Keegan	W.	Sheriff Landis
24.	Julie Michaels	X.	Officer Bish
25.	Adam Marcus	Y.	Elizabeth Marcus (Female agent)
26.	Blake Conway	AA.	Agent Abernathy
27.	James Gleason	BB.	Officer Andell
28.	Billy Green Bush	CC.	Crighton Duke

77

B. Questions: Answer the questions about the movie.

29.   What was Jason's sister's name?
30.   At the beginning of the movie what happened to Jason?
31.   Who eats Jason's heart?
32.   How many people survived?
33.   Who survived?
34.   How many people were killed?
35.   What kind of job did Diana have?
36.   Who played the FBI agent #2?
37.   How did he get killed?
38.   Who produced the movie?
39.   What color was the car that the female FBI agent drove to Crystal Lake?
40.   Whose house was she in when the light bulb melts?
41.   Does she screw in the new light bulb properly?
42.   What color was her jacket?
43.   What happens when she is about to get in the bathtub?
44.   What color towel does she wear when she exits the bathroom?
45.   Who chases her?
46.   Whose blood is on her towel?
47.   Who was the bounty hunter?
48.   Does Agent Markus get injured?
49.   What color tie does the Coroner wear?
50.   Did the Coroner wear a watch?
51.   What color is the Coroner's jacket?
52.   What did the Coroner guess that Jason weighed?
53.   Was Jason's head and heart in one piece?
54.   How large is Jason's heart?
55.   What does the Coroner do with the heart?
56.   What happens to the Coroner?
57.   What pizza place is the dinner ordered from?
58.   What happens to the second Coroner?
59.   What happens to the two security guards?
60.   How many confirmed murders did Jason commit?
61.   What were the names of Jason's parents?
62.   What drink does Creighton Duke have?
63.   What does Creighton Duke say about the real Jason Voorhees?

64. What color of vest does Creighton Duke wear?
65. How much money does Creighton Duke get paid for his services?
66. What is the waitress' name?
67. What color was the vehicle that Steven was driving?
68. What did Diana want to tell Steven?
69. What did Creighton Duke order at the diner?
70. What time did Steven have to meet Diana?
71. What joke does Steven speak of?
72. How many teenagers are at Crystal Lake?
73. What happened to the sign at Crystal Lake?
74. What happened to the cabins at Crystal Lake?
75. What color is the tent that the teenagers are in?
76. Is the moon full or nearly full?
77. What is the blonde Alexis wearing when she is murdered?
78. What color plaid is Deborah wearing for a blouse?
79. What did Jason step on as he roamed to the tent?
80. What color was it?
81. Who was Tango?
82. What color is Diana's uniform?
83. What is Deborah doing when she is killed?
84. How did Edna get killed?
85. Whose arms did Diana die in?
86. How many people in this movie got possess by Jason's spirit?
87. Who is Jessica?
88. Who does Diana see in the mirror?
89. Is Josh the Sheriff?
90. What happened to Deborah?
91. How was she killed?
92. Who was the second person to be possessed by Jason's spirit?
93. Who was Diana talking to on the phone before she gets cut off?
94. What happened to Josh by the fireplace?
95. Who is Stephanie?
96. Whose baby is a Voorhees?
97. Who is cleaning up bloodstains?
98. What is the babysitter's name?
99. Who is placed in jail for Diana's murder?

100. Who gets their fingers broken?
101. Why is Creighton Duke in jail?
102. What can Jessica and her baby do to or for Jason?
103. Who gets their service revolver stolen from them?
104. Who says, "You should have closed up after the funeral"?
105. Did Josh disappear or did he die?
106. Where does the head waitress put the baby?
107. What number and letter is on Steven's jacket?
108. What is in a book that Steven picks up?
109. Who is on the cell phone that is wearing suspenders?
110. What happens when Jessica is in the shower?
111. What does Jessica grab in the dark?
112. Where is she holding the flashlight?
113. What happens to Robert Campbell?
114. Why does Robert Campbell live?
115. What does Jessica do to Steven?
116. Who is Randy?
117. Who is the third person to be possessed by Jason's spirit?
118. Why do Randy and Steven fight?
119. Who slams down a phone?
120. How many shots does Steven fire?
121. What happens to Officers Mark and Brian?
122. Who rushed in and found Steven over Diana's body with blood on his pants and hands?
123. Who calls the sheriff?
124. Who is Ward?
125. Who gets slugged when she guards a baby?
126. What does Robert do to the head waitress?
127. What happens to Ward?
128. What happens to Joey?
129. How did Vicki die?
130. Why does Creighton Duke hold Jessica's baby?
131. What kind of window is next to the front door of the Voorhees house?
132. Who is given the family dagger to kill Jason?
133. Who gave Steven the keys to his car at the diner?
134. Where does Steven go?
135. Who does Jessica kill?

136. What does Randy do to the baby?
137. How is Jason reborn (through whom)?
138. Who does the demon (Jason) possess before he is reborn?
139. Where is the dagger?
140. What happens to Creighton Duke when he tries to kill Jason?
141. How many times does Jason get hit in the head by the shovel?
142. How does Jason go to hell?
143. How many demons grab Steven?
144. How many hands grab Jason?
145. Who grabs the half-buried mask?
146. Name the cut scenes.
147. Name the bloopers.
148. What was added after the first screenings?
149. What was the name of the diner that Diana worked at?
150. What did the sign say at the morgue?
151. At the beginning of the movie, how many bursts of light come out of Jason and into the coroner?
152. Where was the morgue that Jason's remains were sent to?
153. What was the name of the morgue?
154. Name everybody that was killed and how they were killed.
155. How did the coroner describe Jason's heart?
156. What did Creighton Duke tell Jessica about destroying Jason?
157. What is the name of Jason's hometown?
158. How many lights escape from Jason at the end?
159. How was Diana murdered?
160. How old was Jason when he supposedly drowned at Camp Crystal Lake?
161. What were the hamburgers at the diner shaped like?
162. What was the special at the diner?
163. Name the four people that were possessed by Jason's spirit?
164. Does the sheriff get killed too?
165. Who directed this movie?
166. What did Jason do to Josh, (Jason's spirit was in the coroner's body) before he possessed Josh?
167. Who was Diana talking to on the phone before she was killed?
168. Who's arms did Diana die in?
169. Who was possessed by Jason's spirit when he killed Diana?
170. Where did Steven go after Ward gives him the keys to his car?

81

171. Who stole Diana's body from the morgue?
172. Where did he put it?
173. Did Jessica and Steven kiss at the end of the movie?
174. Where there any off-scene kills?
175. How many off-screen kills were there?
176. Who was killed off-screen?
177. When did filming for this movie begin?
178. Who was the producer of this movie?
179. Who was the stunt coordinator?
180. Who was the director of this movie?
181. Who was the music by?
182. Was the movie poster a double-sided poster?
183. Who distributed the movie?
184. When was this movie released?
185. When the coroner's assistant entered the room where the coroner was examining the remains of Jason's body (after he got possessed by Jason's spirit) what was he carrying?
186. Which FBI agent searches the coroner's assistant?
187. After they blew up Jason, the camera shows Creighton Duke standing there, what does he say?
188. What weapon did Jason have in his hand when he frightened the female FBI agent?
189. Which hand did he hold the machete in?
190. When the first guy fired at Jason, where did it hit him?
191. What did Creighton Duke say that the two words Jason Voorhees makes him think of?
192. What television program was Robert Campbell on?
193. What did the big banner at the diner say?
194. Who turns off the TV that showed the program, American Case File?
195. Did Diana shoot Josh (when he was possessed by Jason)?
196. Where did she shoot him?
197. Who is Creighton Duke?
198. What did Diana say as she walks into the diner looking at the banner?
199. Who fought in front of a fireplace?
200. What did Steven stab Josh (when he was possessed by Jason's spirit) with?

201. What did the note say that was for Jessica from Creighton Duke?
202. When the female FBI agent passed a sign, how many miles to Crystal Lake was on the sign?
203. What other towns or cities were on the sign?
204. What did it say on the box of light bulbs, that the female FBI agent got out of the tool shed?
205. What watt of bulbs were they?
206. When she was in the tool shed, what happened?
207. Did it scare her?
208. When the female FBI agent went to take a bath, what was on the shower curtain?
209. When Jason was being shot, near the beginning of the movie, did he make any noise?
210. How did officers Mark and Brian die?
211. How did they destroy Jason near the beginning of the movie?
212. When Jason was reborn through his dead sister, did he have a weapon in his hand?
213. What weapon was it?
214. Which hand was he holding the weapon?
215. How long was the filming schedule for?
216. When did filming begin?
217. Did Kane Hodder have a cameo appearance in this movie?
218. Who did he play?
219. Was his character killed by Jason?
220. How tall is Jason?
221. How tall is Kane Hodder?
222. In all, how many murders totaled from all the Friday the 13th's?
223. How many did Jason actually commit from all the Friday the 13th's?
224. What other movie do you see Jason's mask?
225. Is there going to be another Friday the 13th movie?
226. What is the next Friday the 13th movie called?
227. When do they plan to release it?
228. Is that a Friday the 13th?

Answers to Friday the 13th (Part 1) Trivia Questions:

Matching:

1.   P
2.   H
3.   K
4.   F
5.   M
6.   C
7.   A
8.   L
9.   B
10.   O
11.   N
12.   I
13.   G
14.   J
15.   E
16.   D

B. Answers to the Questions:

17.   Alice Hardy
18.   Camp Blood
19.   Barry…in 1958 and in the present day…Annie
20.   Two in 1958…seven people in the present day (and Mrs. Voorhees makes it eight)
21.   Alice Hardy
22.   Pamela Voorhees
23.   Ari Lehman
24.   Hunting knife in the stomach
25.   Alice was attacked by a muck covered Jason and pulled under the water…in a dream?
26.   Any of the following…Did you know a young boy drowned, the year before those two others were killed? The counselors

weren't paying any attention. They were making love while that poor boy drowned. His name was Jason. I was working the day that it happened, preparing meals here. I was the cook. Jason stood and watched every minute! He was...he wasn't a very good swimmer. We can go now, dear. You see, Jason was my son, and today is his birthday, Oh, I couldn't let them open this place again, could I? Not after what happened. Oh, my sweet innocent Jason. My only child, Jason. You let him drown; you never paid any attention! What you did to him...Look what you did to him!

27. Steve Christy
28. Arrow through he bed and neck.
29. Crazy Ralph and then the truck drive, Enos.
30. It's got a "Death Curse" and it's "Jinxed".
31. Annie
32. She unknowingly hitched a ride with the killer.
33. June 13
34. 1957
35. Jason Voorhees
36. His mother was preparing meals...she was the cook.
37. Pamela Voorhees
38. Crazy Ralph
39. Adrienne King
40. Mrs. Voorhees
41. Decapitated with a machete.
42. Brenda
43. Annie's
44. Peter Brouwer
45. Betsy Palmer
46. Enos
47. a blue jeep
48. Sgt. Tierney
49. Rex Everhart
50. Robbi Morgan
51. Kevin Bacon
52. Mark Nelson
53. Harry Crosby
54. Jeannine Taylor

55. Laurie Bartram
56. rainy and stormy night
57. Blairstown, New Jersey
58. Here are the Bloopers:

1. Annie says she hates it when people call children "kids", but earlier she said that she'll be cooking for 50 kids and seven or eight staff.

2. When everyone is looking for the snake under the bed, Alice first lifts up the sheet and then in the next shot it is Marcie lifting the sheet and Alice is behind her.

3. When Alice is scared, by Crazy Ralph in the pantry she screams and Marcie and Ned come running in. Ned is eating a hamburger but it is only in the next scene that they are preparing the hamburgers in the kitchen.

4. The lightning on Marcie and Jack is obviously not lightning. Lighting has a blue tinge, and it's obvious a large yellow light was flashed at their faces.

5. When Jack gets a spear through his neck, look closely at his neck and you can see the line between Jack's head and the fake chest.

6. When Marcie goes to look behind the shower curtain, a large line was up the left side of the film.

7. Outside the diner it is obviously a fire hose being sprayed back and forth to cause the rain.

8. Why would Brenda walk all the way through the rain to the communal bathroom only to brush her teeth and wash her face when a sink is clearly shown in her own cabin.

9. When Brenda goes out into the rain because she hears a voice, it is definitely a child's voice that says, "Help me please, Heeelp!" You can hear the voice break like a child's something Mrs. Voorhees could not and does no do.

10. When we see the axe on the pillow there is blood on only one side. Why would Mrs. Voorhees have cleaned one side of the axe?

11. While Alice is alone making coffee on a table behind her is a blender and to the right of the blender is sitting a basket of eggs. When Alice returns to the kitchen (after

discovering Bill's body) the blender and eggs have switched places.

12. When Alice discovers Bill's body hanging on the door, his right eye twitches slightly.

13. Brenda's head moves after she is thrown through the window, after we assure she is dead.

Explanation: Either she is not completely dead or her head is just settling.

14. After Brenda is thrown through the window, Alice quickly bolts out of the room and throws open the door. As she was out of the cabin, Mrs. Voorhees pulls up in the jeep. Even had Mrs. Voorhees pushed Brenda through the window, jumped into the jeep and then came down to the cabin from the front, Alice would have heard it.

15. When Mrs. Voorhees is telling Alice about Jason drowning, you can see a small camp fire outside through the window. Who had the time (and was alive) to make a fire in the wind?

16. When Alice finds Steve's body, his wound has moved from his stomach to his chest.

17. Mrs. Voorhees arm change position when she is lying on the ground after being hit by Alice with the frying pan. She falls down with her arms above her head but then her left arm is lying on her chest in the next shot.

18. When Alice screams and "swings the machete into the left side of Pamela's neck. But the neck opens up on Pamela's right side, making it look like Alice has just knocked Mrs. Voorhees head off.

19. After Alice chops Mrs. Voorhees' head off, as she's about to get in the canoe she turns around and stares right at the camera for 1 or 2 seconds.

20. The movie is supposed to take place in the summer, but right before Jason jumps up and attacks Alice, in the background the leaves on the trees are fall colors.

21. When Alice is in the hospital, the nurse standing to the left flicks her eyes to the camera.

22. When Claudette and the counselors are singing in the beginning, the close-ups of Claudette show her legs crossed, but the far-away shots show her legs spread apart.

23. Also, when Claudette finishes playing the guitar, the music continues after she stops strumming the stings.

24. If you look at Claudette's socks as she leaves the cabin, they are pulled up to just about the middle of her calves. However, when she enters the barn with Barry shortly after, the top her socks are folded down so that they appear to be just above her ankles.

25. After Steve, Marcy, Ned and Jack get the tree stump out of the ground near the lake, Alice joins them and puts a bucket she is carrying down on the ground. In the next shot, Alice is again seen putting the bucket down.

26. When Steve is talking to Alice outside of the cabin, he reaches up and rests his hands on the gutter. After the reverse shot of Alice, both of his arms are at his sides.

27. When Annie trips in the forest and is bucking up against the tree, in each shot her hair is in different positions with varying amounts of leaves in it.

28. Crazy Ralph had propped his bicycle against a tree post outside the front door of the cabin. Why didn't anybody notice his bike sitting right out there in the open?

29. Just before Jack's death, he is smoking a joint and both of his arms are out in front of him. When it cuts to the side shot of him being stabbed both of arms are stiffly at his sides.

30. When Sgt. Tierney is giving Steve a ride, he gets a call on his radio. As he is replacing the receiver, he flips on the lights. In the next shot, the siren lights are off and then they are switched on again.

31. When Alice runs to the boathouse where she gets the gun, there are several pieces of wood leaning against it outside to the right. As Alice opens the door and slips inside, one piece of wood falls over diagonally. In subsequent outside shots of the door, the piece of wood is in its original position.

59.   Here are the cut scenes:
    1. A more graphic scene of Jack's (Kevin Bacon's) knifing. Blood spits out all over his clothes. His eyes bug out a bit more.
    2. Marcie is axed in the face with more force, hits the wall and lays for a few more seconds than in the version shown.
    3. Claudette is an onscreen kill. She is knifed in the neck.

60.   Here is everybody and how they were killed:
    1. Barry - Knifed in the stomach.
    2. Claudette - Knifed off-screen.
    3. Annie - Throat slashed with a hunting knife.
    4. Ned - Throat slashed.
    5. Jack - Arrow through his bed and neck.
    6. Marcie - Axed in the face.
    7. Brenda - Killed off-screen, later thrown through a window.
    8. Steve Christy-hunting knife in the stomach.
    9. Bill - Pinned to a door with arrows.
    10. Mrs. Voorhees - Decapitated with a machete.
61.   Ron Carroll
62.   Ned, Jack and Marcie
63.   Alice
64.   Bill and then a few minutes later, Ned, Jack and Marcie.
65.   Bill
66.   a machete
67.   Right hand, ring finger.
68.   Muck from the bottom of Crystal Lake.
69.   Camp Blood
70.   Because of all the killings there.
71.   Officer Dorf
72.   Ned
73.   Four people
74.   Removing a tree stump
75.   Painting
76.   By the lake.
77.   Steve wants to know if we need more paint.
78.   her drawings

79. Alice hit Mrs. Voorhees with:
    1. a small rifle (used it like a baseball bat)
    2. threw a ball of twine, and an assortment of wood working tools, and a .22 caliber gun
    3. a heavy skillet
    4. finally a machete and decapitates her

80. "I'm Mrs.Voorhees, an old friend of the Christys'"
81. Blue
82. Blue
83. a machete
84. Sgt. Tierney's men
85. The boy Jason Voorhees…the one who attacked Alice and the one who pulled her under the water.
86. Steve Christy's
87. Brenda
88. Sgt. Tierney
89. his jeep broke down and it was raining
90. Blue Jean Cut-Offs
91. Everybody contributed in helping to save Ned (Bill, Alice, Brenda, Jack and Marcie)
92. Looks like it's gonna rain like hell, so get as much done as possible. I don't wanna get too far behind.
93. Talking to the killer; like he knew the person
94. "Oh hi, what are you doing out in this mess"?
95. Dark Brown
96. yes, barely…but no one saw him
97. Checking the emergency generator
98. a red and white handkerchief
99. no
100. 1958
101. 2
102. 20 miles
103. 347-1063
104. Enos
105. red
106. Camp Crystal Lake is jinxed…and to quit

107. It wasn't working out at the camp and she had business to take care of.
108. Ned was wearing a Hawaiian styled shirt with flowers on it when he arrived. Then later, when he scares Brenda at the Archery Range, he is wearing a red, short sleeved T-shirt that has black and white stripes around the sleeves and neck (collar). And then when Alice screams for Bill, because, of the snake she finds in her cabin, he is wearing a green and white shirt with the number 88 on it.
109. bow and arrows
110. Jack
111. He asked if they have seen somebody by the name of Crazy Ralph
112. Bill
113. making out...fornicating
114. Crazy Ralph
115. Alice
116. He says that Crazy Ralph gets drunk and gets his calling and Dorf spends a day in court and Ralph gets a week in jail.
117. Carefully walk a cross it like it is a balancing beam.
118. Yeah, I've had this dream about five or six times where I'm in a thunderstorm, and it's raining really hard. It sounds like pebbles when it hits the ground. I can hear it and I try to block out the sound with my hands and it doesn't work. It just keeps getting louder and louder and then the rain turns to blood and it washes away in little rivers and the sound stops.
119. 6
120. Bill...and then Alice later
121. in the bunk bed above Jack's bunk bed
122. to the bathroom
123. Strip Monopoly
124. Brenda, Alice and Bill
125. Bill
126. Alice
127. Bill
128. Bill
129. Brenda
130. their clothes

131. no
132. Bill
133. Bill
134. Brenda
135. Jack lights a cigarette. Blood drops onto his throat from above. A hand grabs his forehead and an arrow is shoved through his throat from under his bed.
136. unstopped water pipe
137. standing next to 2nd shower curtain
138. axe hits her in the head (in the face)
139. Sandy
140. red
141. green
142. silver
143. Sgt. Tierney
144. White
145. Because she hears a little boy's voice calling out for help.
146. yes
147. she gets killed off screen…but later her dead body is thrown through a window
148. at the Archery range
149. yes
150. reddish-brown
151. Rescue Squad. Wreck near mile marker 17, possible male, three, maybe more, trapped, head on.
152. yellow
153. yes
154. Bill, then Alice
155. Bill
156. Bill, then Alice
157. a tea pot
158. outside and then in the emergency generator room
159. yes
160. she locks herself in the cabin
161. Brenda's
162. She tells Alice about her son Jason that drowned
163. Ned
164. Dark Brown

165.   A gray sweater and black pants
166.   on the banks of Crystal Lake
167.   He told her that his men pulled her out of the lake, they thought that she was dead too.
168.   yes
169.   white
170.   1980, 93 minutes
171.   This is a very controversial question, if there is such a thing in this Friday the 13th series, when Jason jumped out of the lake in part one, it was all an illusion, a dream of Alice's mind. Remember how Renee saw Jason as a young boy in Jason takes in Manhattan when she was on the cruise ship and fell into the water, she saw a young boy attacking her.
172.   Norlittle Cemetery
173.   Cycle 2
174.   1958
175.   1979
176.   yes
177.   Here are the script differences: Did you know that originally the opening sequence of the original Friday the 13th, was supposed to be a big lengthy change scene? Originally, after the murder (Mrs. Voorhees) killed the male counselor in the Barn, this female counselor escaped and was pursued down by the lake and through a boat house. Due to the weather complications the scene had to be bounced.
178.   Crazy Ralph
179.   Because he was a troublemaker
180.   Fires and bad water
181.   1962
182.   The truck driver, Enos
183.   Annie
184.   Sleeping
185.   Bill's
186.   Tom Savini
187.   Stephen Miner
188.   Tom Savini
189.   red
190.   Harry Manfredini

191. yes
192. Baker
193. 1930
194. Pamela Sue
195. Sean S. Cunningham
196. Because she could supply her own transportation.
197. in a basement, with a 12 piece orchestra
198. The River Jordan, Hang Down Your Head Tom Dooley (Tom Dooley)
199. Claudette, Brenda, Ned and Bill
200. 1 not including the killer
201. 7
202. Trudy
203. a year
204. Ned
205. yes
206. yes
207. Speeded up…instead of stopping
208. she jumped out of the speeding car
209. Go into the woods
210. yes
211. She gets killed by the stranger in the woods.
212. Throat slashed with a hunting knife.
213. Robbie Morgan
214. Ned
215. Marcie
216. Rocky Road
217. Camp Crystal Lake Established in 1935.
218. Yellow with Green and Red Letters
219. "Do you remember much?"
220. Is there anybody left alive? Are they all dead?
221. The boy Jason
222. Bill
223. Pinned to a door with arrows
224. Harry Crosby
225. A trailer
226. Because the wind blew the door open and blew their playing pieces everywhere

227. An Axe
228. The Bathroom
229. Alice
230. Bill
231. The phone lines were cut in two
232. No
233. It looked like Ned, Jack and Marcie's
234. 20 miles
235. Gray with a black band around the middle of his hat
236. Yes
237. Her leg
238. yes
239. yes
240. Slashed her throat with a hunting knife.
241. Steve Christy
242. Paint Thinner
243. 25,000 dollars
244. The truck driver Enos
245. Annie
246. Dorothy Kobbs
247. The killer's feet
248. Alice
249. Cabin B
250. Annie
251. 50 kids and staff
252. yes
253. The Cross-roads
254. Sean Cunningham
255. June 13th, 1980
256. under $500,000
257. $40,000
258. Midnight on Friday June 13th, 1946
259. Elias Todd Voorhees
260. 11 years old
261. yes
262. yes
263. Ned

264. Ned was wearing his green shirt wrapped around his bottom like a diaper and his white underwear was showing and an Indian feather headdress
265. Brenda and Marcie
266. Betsy Palmer, Adrienne King, Harry Crosby, Kevin Bacon, Ari Lehman
267. yes
268. I think we better wait for Mr. Christy
269. They shouldn't have opened this place again.
270. "Ma'am we didn't find any boy."
271. "Then he's still there."
272. yes
273. A motorcycle
274. Yes
275. Ari Lehman
276. 7:01 am
277. A muck covered Jason jumping out of Crystal Lake and bringing a unhappy camper down with him.
278. 1930
279. yes
280. a particular spot of Crystal Lake where Jason pulled Alice under
281. Friday The 13th: Long Night At Camp Blood
282. When Sean S. Cunningham started Production on it.
283. So it would be like Halloween
284. Sean S. Cunningham
285. Tom Savini
286. yes (Part 4) The Final Chapter
287. Brown
288. Annie's
289. Steve Christy's
290. Brenda
291. Bill's

Answers for Friday The 13th (Part 2) Trivia Questions:

A. Matching:

1. K
2. O
3. N
4. P
5. H
6. M
7. Q
8. C
9. D
10. E
11. A
12. J
13. I
14. B
15. F
16. G
17. L

B. Answers to the Questions about the movie:

18.   Alice
19.   Ice pick through he temple
20.   Right after she was in the hospital and the sheriff tells her that they didn't find any boy and then she Says "Then he's still there"
21.   Orange and white
22.   2
23.   3 months
24.   The Itsy Bitsy Spider
25.   Jason's mother's decapitated head
26.   Her parents and a little later on an obscene phone caller?
27.   Feed her cat

28. She dreamed of that horrible night of Friday the 13th at Camp Crystal Lake, when she was the only survivor
29. Her cat
30. Kitchen
31. Mrs.   Voorhees
32. Yes
33. Warrington Gillette
34. 5 years
35. Jeff and Sandra
36. Ginny
37. Car trouble?
38. Motorcycle accident
39. Machete in the face
40. Crazy Ralph
41. He gets killed
42. Garroted with a barb wire
43. He was spying on Ginny and Paul
44. The cut Scenes are:
    1. A close-up shot of the couple (Jeff and Sandra) being impaled while having sex on a bed.
    2. The wire up close cutting Crazy Ralph.

45. The Bloopers are:
    1. Jason is still 11 at the end of the original when he emerged from the lake (after twenty or so years). If there were only five years in between the first and the second films, how could Jason have become full-grown especially since he hadn't grown at all while in the lake?

       EXPLANATION: Alice was not physically attacked by Jason, it was a dream or psychic vision.

    2. When Alice gets in the shower, it seems the time it takes her is way too short, even for just rinsing off. She seems to end her shower right before the phone rings, and it appeared as if she was getting out any way.

EXPLANATION: Pay attention. Her opening the curtain and getting out occur at different times. The phone ringing is an audio segue that leads you to think the shots are subsequent, but she is not actually getting out when she opens the curtain. It's a "gotcha" where she looks right at the camera.

3. When Alice gets out of the shower her hair is fully dry.
4. In the prologue, when Alice is scared by a cat "jumping" in the window. It is apparent the cat was actually thrown through the window by a crewmember.
5. When Crazy Ralph is strangled with the wire, the wire is placed over the tree and around his neck which seems quite strange considering the tree would be too tall to reach over.
6. The Sheriff leaves his car in the middle of the road when he gets out to chase Jason, but when Ginny and Paul come back that night, Jason sure has done a good job of hiding a bright white police car in the dark woods.
7. When Jason slits Scott's throat the machete cuts his Neck straight across - yet the wound is diagonal.
8. When Paul offers the counselors a last night on the town, he claims "We've only got two cars", but later Vicki goes to hers to get a hairbrush. Wouldn't they have borrowed hers instead of Ginny's old clunker?
9. When Mark gets the machete in the face, the camera cuts to a far shot. In the first shot, he is in the middle of the porch and Jason is right behind him. When it shows the front, he is right on the stairs, and Jason is nowhere to be seen.
10. When Mark is machetied in the face, Jason hits Mark's face from the right side with the handle down, yet when he's going down the stairs backwards the handle is now on the top left side of his face.
11. When Ginny is hiding in front of the car her head is visible above the hood (see her shadow on top of it), where Jason could see it from where he is walking.

12. When Jason is in Ginny's cabin you can see the mike wire's shadow on the floor when he starts walking towards the cots.
13. If Muffin came back at the end, then what dog (with a purple bow!) did Sandra and Jeff find the remains of in the woods?
14. What happened to the rest of the counselors at the bar? Did they stay out the entire night? Not one of them is seen at the camp in the morning.
15. Mrs. Voorhees in Part 1 had short puffy -like hair, but she had longer straight hair in Part 2 when they show the head.
16. At the end of Part 2 when Jason is unmasked. He has some hair but is mostly bald. His face looks horrible and his eyes don't line up, his skin is grayish, etc. Again in Part 3, Jason is unmasked he looks totally different. The action; in these films, are separated by a matter of minutes…yet his look has been altered.
17. At the end, when Jason jumps through the window and grabs Ginny. Well in that part he still has the machete sticking out of his arm. Then at the beginning of part 3, when they replay the end of part 2 again, they show Ginny takes off Jason's Mask, after she hits him in the shoulder with the machete. Then after Ginny and Paul walk out of the shack, the camera shows Jason (still lying on the floor) pull the machete out of his arm and crag himself off camera.

46.   Paul
47.   Terri
48.   Muffin
49.   Claw hammer to the back of his head
50.   In the oldest cabin deep in the woods of Camp Crystal Lake, looking at the shrine for Jason's mother (her decapitated head)
51.   "Oh My God"
52.   A counselor training camp near Camp Crystal Lake
53.   Sandra, Jeff, Mark, Vicki, Terri and Scott
54.   Paul
55.   Paul, Ginny, Ted and some other people not named

56. Ginny and Paul
57. Her parents and a while later, an obscene phone caller
58. In the left shoulder
59. A machete
60. Ginny runs in the woods, trying to get away from Jason and finds, an old run down cabin in the middle of the woods. She enters it and then tries to hide from Jason in one of the rooms which is Jason's shrine and then she tries to pretend that she's Jason's mom that has been brought back from the dead and it almost works. Then Paul finds her, and fights with Jason and the Ginny hits Jason in the left shoulder with a Machete, and then Paul and Ginny go back to their cabin and then Terri's little dog comes to the cabin door. And right behind Ginny, as she reaches for the little dog...through the window, Jason smashes through and attacks her. It flashes to her being taken away by the paramedic and her calling out for Paul.
61. Ted
62. Someone towing their truck away.
63. a mouse
64. She wet herself
65. Yes
66. On a chair
67. A pitchfork
68. Yes
69. Yes
70. Before the last scene, John Furey quit
71. A gunny sack
72. Ted
73. 5
74. At the end when he breaks through the window and attacks Ginny
75. Fields
76. Scott
77. He walks right into a snare trap and is swinging upside down...Terri runs to get a knife to cut him loose and Jason kills Scott before she gets back.
78. A mangled up animal, it's too mangled up to tell what it is, they think it's a dog

79. Jason Voorhees is the legend of Camp Crystal Lake.
80. A shrine to his mother
81. Holt
82. Jason's mother
83. His mother's sweater
84. Paul
85. He pulled the gunnysack off of Jason's head while he laid unconscious after Ginny hits him in the shoulder with the machete.
86. "Jesus"
87. A pitchfork
88. On a chair, in her cabin
89. The chair breaks and Jason falls and the pitchfork that he was holding breaks in half.
90. A chainsaw and then hits him with a wooden chair.
91. It started raining right after Vicki went to her car for a hairbrush for her "meeting" with Mark.
92. Right after it starts raining well actually if you listen when Mark and Vicki are discussing about what cabin to use it starts way in the background, very lightly and then you don't hear anything until Vicki goes to get her hair brush from the car.
93. A hair brush
94. Jeff's
95. Jeff and Sandra
96. Knifed
97. Vicki's
98. Ginny
99. Paul
100. Yes
101. 2
102. A big log
103. No
104. A pick axe
105. On her leg…right leg
106. Jeff and Sandra
107. A broken old sign of Camp Crystal Lake
108. Calling Ted (Using a pay phone)

109. "I told the others and they didn't believe me...you're all doomed, you're all doomed."
110. They were not allowed to go into town, when everybody else did, for a last night out.
111. Ginny
112. Paul
113. No
114. His Mother
115. Yes
116. No
117. Paul
118. 2
119. Crazy Ralph
120. He forgot to shut his car door
121. Jeff and Sandra - doubled impaled with a spear.
122. 11
123. Pack-a-nack Counselor Training Center.
124. The bars name was Casino
125. The Smokey Boys Band
126. 577-BOC
127. Black
128. The Country Grocer
129. He said, "It was Bear Country"
130. Amy Steel
131. Yellow
132. 13
133. Exxon
134. "I don't want to scare anyone; but, I'm going to give it to you straight about Jason," his body was never recovered from the lake after he drowned. And if you listen to the old timers in town, they'll tell you he's still out there, some sort of demented creature surviving in the wilderness, full grown by now, stalking...stealing what he needs...living off wild animals and vegetation...some...some folks claimed they've seen him. Right in this area. The girl who survived that night at "Camp Blood," that Friday The 13th...she claims she saw him...she disappeared 2 months later, vanished...blood was everywhere...no one knows what happened to her. Legend

has it that Jason saw his mother beheaded that night and he took his revenge, a revenge that he would return here...5 years, 5 long years he's been dormant. And he's hungry. Jason's out there, watching, always on the prowl for intruders, ready to kill, ready to devour, thirsty for young blood."

135. Ted
136. A mask and animal skins around him like a native headhunter or something
137. A spear
138. Left hand
139. Sandra
140. Amy Steel accidentally cuts off the Jason stunt double's finger with a machete during a fight scene.
141. Steve Daskawitz
142. Vicki's
143. At the beginning of the movie when Alice decapitated Jason's mother and near the end when Ginny hits Jason with the machete and when Jason smashed through the window and attacks Ginny.
144. Muffin was white and beige and gray.
145. Everybody was swimming and having a good time in the lake.
146. Ginny
147. What's green and red and goes 100 miles an hour?
148. A frog in a blender.
149. What's brown and sits on a piano?
150. Beethoven's Last Movement
151. Jason
152. Jason
153. She hid in the room that Jason's shrine was in along with his mother's decapitated head and all of the dead bodies of his victims.
154. Pick Axe
155. yes
156. Steve Miner
157. These people produced this movie: Lisa Barsamian (executive), Frank Mancuso Jr. (Associate), Steve Miner, Dennis Murphy (co-producer)
158. Cliff Cudney

159. Harry Manfredini
160. 1981
161. 8
162. Carl Fullerton
163. Paramount Pictures
164. Yes
165. 10 million
166. 87 minutes
167. The part of a broken pitch fork, the sharp end
168. Betsy Palmer, Amy Steel, John Furey, Adrienne King and Warrington Gillette as Jason
169. Most memorable murder: A tomahawk goes through the bodies of two fornicating youths.
170. Jeff and Sandra's
171. Right as she and Paul leave the old rundown shack of a cabin in the middle of the woods.
172. His Friday turn-ons included a chance to jump through windows.
173. Turn-offs: artificial teeth, 6-hour makeup sessions, and all-night shooting.
174. A whistling tea kettle
175. Paul there's somebody in this room. Paul there is somebody in this fucking room.
176. Ginny pretends to be Jason's mom, to try to fool him and it doesn't work. And then Paul rescued her and then Paul and Jason fight and then Ginny hits Jason in the left shoulder with a machete and Paul unmasks Jason and then they leave and a little while later, Jason busts through a window. Surprising the 2 victims, Paul and Ginny.
177. Ginny
178. Here is everybody in order and how they were killed:
    1. Alice - Stabbed in the temple with an ice pick.
    2. Crazy Ralph - Garroted with barbed wire.
    3. Policeman - Claw hammer in the head.
    4. Scott - Throat slashed while hanging in a snare.
    5. Terry - Knifed
    6. Mark - Machete in the face.
    7. Jeff and Sandra - Double impaling with a spear.

8. Vickie - Knifed

9. Paul - Disappeared, presumed dead.

179. The little dog, Muffin
180. The handle of the broken pitch fork.
181. Paul
182. The little dog, Muffin
183. She goes and takes a shower
184. Kent, Connecticut
185. yes
186. Max
187. Carl Fullerton
188. Because the roll of Jason had less impact than he'd hoped for.
189. No
190. Paul
191. 15? - 20?
192. Her revenge, her sense of loss, her rage of what she thought happened, her love for Jason
193. Paul
194. Tom McBride
195. Mark (The guy in the wheel chair)
196. Ted
197. Terri
198. Yes
199. Ginny
200. Yes
201. Ted
202. Her little dog, Muffin
203. Around where he had his mom's head, a shrine for her, in hopes for a resurrection, and around his mother's decapitated head he placed 13 candles.
204. 1980
205. Yes
206. 10 million
207. Yes
208. In the main cabin and the old run-down shack in the woods.
209. Terri
210. Paul

211. Yes
212. David Brand, China Chen, Carolyn Louden, Jaimie Perry, Tom Shea and Jill Voight
213. Jeff's
214. Francis Warrington Gillette
215. No
216. Black
217. Vicki
218. Amy Steel
219. Produced and Directed by Steve Miner
220. Ginny...Amy Steel
221. Extra Counselors: David Brand, China Chen, Carolyn Louden, Jaimie Perry, Tom Shea and Jill Voight
222. No
223. No
224. Jerry Wallace
225. Steve Daskawitz
226. You want something to eat?
227. By the door in the old run down cabin
228. Jason, It's all done Jason, you've done your job well and mommy is please. That's a good boy. Now come to mommy, come on, come on, Mommy has a reward for you. Jason, mother is talking to you, come on, that's my boy, come, kneel down, that's a good boy, kneel down, that's my good boy, that's a good boy, good Jason.
229. Red
230. Volkswagon Convertible
231. Black
232. Max
233. Paul
234. her cat
235. Hello? Somebody please help me
236. Crazy Ralph
237. Ted
238. Terry
239. Jeff and Sandra
240. Green with white trim and a black roof.
241. 4 weeks

Answers for Friday the 13th Part 3 Trivia Questions

A. Matching:

1.   F
2.   H
3.   R
4.   G
5.   A
6.   J
7.   L
8.   O.
9.   M
10.   N
11.   E
12.   D
13.   K
14.   C
15.   Q
16.   B
17.   P
18.   I

B. Answer to the questions about the movie:

19.   7 kids and 3 bikers
20.   Chris
21.   Richard Brooker
22.   Higgins Haven
23.   Summer
24.   Chris
25.   Hit in the head with an axe
26.   Shelly
27.   Shelly was killed off screen, later found with his throat slashed
28.   Yes

29. Shelly
30. Vera and Shelly
31. Rick's
32. Ali, Loco and Fox
33. In the barn at Higgins Haven
34. Ali
35. Chopped his hand off with a machete and machetied him to death.
36. In the barn at Higgins Haven
37. She hits him in the head (left side, it cut threw the Hockey mask into his head)
38. Ali
39. Rick's
40. Chris
41. Yes
42. In the barn at Higgins Haven
43. (1)
44. Here is everybody and how they were killed:
    1. Harold - cleaver in the chest.
    2. Edna - knitting needle in the back of the head.
    3. Fox - pitchfork through the neck onto a rafter.
    4. Loco - pitchfork in the stomach.
    5. Ali - bludgeoned with a wrench; later revives and is machetied.
    6. Shelly - killed off-screen, later found with his throat slashed.
    7. Vera - spear gunned in the eye.
    8. Andy - machetied in half while walking on his hands.
    9. Debbie - knifed from beneath her hammock.
    10. Chuck - electrocuted on a fuse box.
    11. Chili - stabbed with a fire place poker.
    12. Rick - head squeezed till his eye pops out.

45. Here are the Bloopers from this movie:
    1. When Jason at the end is being stabbed in the leg, by Amy you can see that the knife hits his left leg, but he pulls out the knife from his right leg.

2. When Shelly and Vera are walking out of the store, Vera stuffs Shelly's wallet into her beige pants while sitting on the dock, she pulls them out of her pink pants (what were they color change pants?)

3. When the girl tells Chris to stop the van so they don't hit the man, if you look in the back, Shelly and the others are not in the back of the van.

4. You can see the wire it is attached to the snake jumping in the cage (at the beginning) and the eyeball, popping scene.

5. During the "arrow shot" scene, where the girl gets shot in the eye, you can see the wire it is attached to.

6. When Fox gets the pitchfork through her neck she is stuck on the rafter but later when Chris is in the upstairs barn Fox's body is nowhere to be found.

7. At the end of Part 2, Paul survives with Ginny. In Part 3 they show Ginny and they say she is the only survivor.

8. Jason has no apparent wound where he was knifed in the shoulder the day before.

9. While Chili is handing Andy a joint, the way she is holding it changes from shot to shot.

46. Here are the Cut Scenes from this movie:
    1. A more graphic death of Andy. His right leg and part of his stomach is taken off.
    2. Vera's spear gun in the eyeshot is longer with more of a reaction shot. It was cut because the ratings board said it looked too real.
    3. An alternated ending in which Chris walks out into the cabin after hitting Jason with the axe. As she walks in she sees Jason. He raises his machete, and he slices her head clean off of her shoulders, takes her head right off. Chris then wakes up in the cop car as usual.
    4. Shelly's death was cut, so he was killed off-screen.

47. Ali

48. Ali breaks the driver's window and breaks the windshield with a chain wrapped around his fist.

49. Walking on his hands, to go get Debbie and himself a beer.

50. (2)
51. Harold and Edna
52. (12)
53. In the barn at Higgins Haven.
54. Rick
55. Shelly
56. Debbie and Andy
57. Vera Sanchez
58. Chris
59. An arrow flies through the air into an eyeball (Vera's murder).
60. A log from the woodpile.
61. In the back of the head.
62. She rolls up his hands in the van window, which had Jason stopped for the moment.
63. He smashed the window with his Hockey Masked face.
64. Way up on a rafter near the ceiling.
65. She dropped down and lands on top of him, knocking him flat.
66. Jason's dead mother, Pamela Voorhees
67. A machete
68. Debbie's
69. She screamed when she was in the closet after finding Debbie's dead body and she gasped a bit too loudly.
70. a knife
71. In his left leg, above the knee.
72. Paul and Jason
73. A machete
74. Ginny and Paul
75. Ginny
76. Her leg was cut by Jason.
77. She was attacked by Jason.
78. Through the broken window.
79. An axe.
80. Because of a rattlesnake was in it's cage.
81. her knitting needle
82. Lyonel
83. dead fly eggs
84. a chocolate doughnut
85. (3)

86. peanuts, orange juice and a doughnut
87. (8)
88. Ginny Fields
89. Steve Miner, the guy that directed Part 2 and Part 3
90. Police
91. A canoe and some bags
92. Shelly
93. at the store
94. Loco
95. Fox - pitchfork through the neck onto a rafter.
96. Loco - pitchfork in the stomach.
97. Ali
98. Andy and Shelly
99. Shelly was juggling apples and Andy was juggling oranges.
100. Shelly's wallet
101. She had forgotten to give it back to him earlier.
102. Rick
103. Chili
104. Dressing in a wet suit and wearing a Hockey mask and going under the water of the lake and grabbing her ankle and scared Vera while she was sitting on the dock.
105. Andy - machete in half while walking on his hands.
106. Chuck
107. Chuck
108. He was pushed by Jason into the fuse box.
109. He said that he was going outside to take a look around.
110. Rick - head squeezed till his eye pops out.
111. Here are the things that Chris did to Jason to try to stop him:
    1. Dumped a bookcase full of books at him.
    2. Stabbed in the right hand.
    3. Stabbed in the left leg.
    4. Hit him with a log in the back of the head.
    5. Almost ran over him, but he darts out of the way in the nick of time.
    6. Rolled up his hands in her van window.
    7. Drops on him from a rafter in the barn and knocks him down.

8. Knocks him out with a shovel and puts the rope around his neck that is on the pulley to lift hay to hay loft in the barn and pushes him off the hay loft of the barn (and he gets hung).

9. Hits him in the head with an axe.

112. She was right outside of the barn.
113. Loco
114. The old man lying in the middle of the road.
115. She screamed because she saw a mouse.
116. Simon Hawke
117. A picture of Shelly and his mom.
118. Greenblatt
119. Chili
120. a chair
121. popcorn
122. The lights were dimming and flashing.
123. The total is $18.50.   We don't accept no food stamps.
124. She was looking at a magazine.
125. Sanchez
126. Bloody clothes and the bathtub was over flowing with water.
127. I don't know if you remember but when you dropped me off that night it was very late. I knew my parents would be waiting for me, but I didn't care. We had such a good time. The minute I walked in the door, my parents started yelling at me and cursing me. We had such a big fight. My mom slapped me. That was the first time that my mom ever hit me. I couldn't believe it, I ran out the door and into the woods. I wanted to punish them. And so I decided to hide out all night. I thought I'd get them so worried that they would be sorry for what they did. And it had been raining in the woods, it was cold and wet. I found a dry spot under an old oak tree. I guess I fell asleep, all I can remember next was being startled out of sleep by the sound of footsteps. I was sure it was dad, so I sat up and listened for him but the footsteps stopped. Then there was this crackling sound behind me I turned around and standing there was this hideous looking man. He was so grotesque, he's almost inhuman. He had a knife and he

attacked me with it. I was so hysterical. I don't know how I was even able to think. But I kicked the knife out of his hands and I ran but he ran after me and he caught me and pulled me down at the ground. I was kicking and screaming and yelling but it didn't do any good, he dragged me along the ground. I blacked out, I don't know what happened after that. I just don't know. When I woke up I was in my own bed. My parents have never said a word about it. They act as if the whole thing never happened but it did. All I want is to just forget it; but, I can't I will never forget that horrible face, never.

128. The show was "Easy Money".
129. The answer was "Charles Dickens"
130. "Fangoria" the spectacular first issue.
131. Chris gets her head chopped off by Jason in a dream sequence.
132. It just says Crystal Lake.
133. He has a fascination for trains.
134. The things that show this are: He has a miniature train in his fish bowl, he has a poster for "The Great Train Robbery" and several other pictures and paintings of trains in his store, and outside where the clothes are hanging there is a sign that reads "Look Out For The Locomotive"
135. (8)
136. (2)
137. Saugas, California
138. yes
139. Steve Miner
140. Lisa Barsamian (Executive), Tony Bishop (Co-Producer), Frank Mancuso Jr. and Peter Schindler (Associate)
141. Harry Manfredini
142. John Sherrod
143. Friday The 13th (Part 3) 3-D and Friday The 13th (Part 3)
144. Martin Kitrosser and Carol Watson
145. Ed Harris (Steve Miner played him)
146. **KLTZ**
147. She was reported in serious condition.
148. Because she wanted to prove that she was stronger than she thought she was.

149. Jason not being dead and after her and Mrs. Voorhees attacking her in the lake.
150. Chief Fittsimmons
151. Yes
152. The barn
153. Yes
154. 1982
155. Paramount Pictures
156. Yes
157. 36 million dollars
158. 4 million dollars budget
159. Pepper
160. (13)
161. Mrs. Voorhees
162. Yes
163. Friday the 13th (Part 3) 3-D
164. Michael Avallone
165. Derek
166. Friday the 13th (Part 3) 3-D
167. Yes
168. A flea market or a used book store
169. Chris, Debbie and Andy
170. Chris
171. No bring her to me.
172. An actor
173. Chris
174. "She is not going"
175. Andy
176. Shelly
177. Debbie
178. Because smoke was coming out of the van.
179. Chili and Chuck
180. A bong filled with Marijuana and Chili and Chuck were puffing away on it.
181. Andy, Shelly, Vera, Debbie Chuck and Chili
182. He was wearing a mask and he went up behind Andy and stabbed Andy with a rubber knife.
183. Andy

184. An asshole
185. I'm not an asshole I'm an actor.
186. Shelly
187. 36 million dollars
188. Dana Kimmel, Paul Kratha
189. Tracie Savage, Jeffrey Rogers, Catherine Parks, Larry Zerner, David Katims, Rachel Howard, and Richard Brooker as Jason.
190. Because of the amount of violence in the film.
191. She was suffering from multiple stab wounds and severe hysterical shock.
192. A rattlesnake almost bit him in the face in his rabbit's cage.
193. Police Chief, Scott Fittsimmons
194. Yes
195. Steve Miner
196. Yes
197. Yes
198. What's wrong? What happened? It's all that crap you've been stuffing yourself with.
199. Chris and her family
200. Marijuana
201. Eat it.
202. It's you
203. (2)
204. (7)
205. Crystal Lake
206. Multiple stab wounds and severe hysterical shock
207. 4 square miles
208. Yes
209. Harold's clothes
210. Yes
211. Vinegar
212. If Edna catches you she'd make a fur coat out of ya.
213. Gray and white
214. Yes
215. Yes
216. What are you so nervous about?
217. Yes
218. A rattlesnake was in the rabbit's cage.

219. In the bathroom
220. Screaming at the sight of a mouse.
221. Yes
222. In the late Spring of 1982.
223. At a ranch in Newhall, CA (about 30 miles north of LA)
224. 12 weeks

Answers for Friday the 13th (Part 4) The Final Chapter

A. Matching:

1.   D
2.   H
3.   A
4.   F
5.   G
6.   B
7.   C
8.   O
9.   E
10. N
11. L
12. I
13. J
14. K
15. M

B. Answer to the questions about the movie:

16.   Rob (In Part 2 Sandra was his sister)
17.   His sister was killed by Jason.
18.   Ted White played Jason, but in the movie he was not given credit.
19.   The Wessex County Morgue
20.   (2)
21.   Tommy Jarvis and his sister Trish.
22.   Tommy
23.   Corey Feldman
24.   Here are the cut scenes from this movie:
   1. The scene where Trish finds the dead body of her mother.
   2. A scene where Tommy shows Rob a fake guillotine.
   3. A scene where Tommy shows Rob a fake severed hand.

4. A scene where Tommy shows Rob a toy soldier melting under a magnifying glass.

25. Pamela Voorhees
26. (13)
27. Yes, Mrs. Jarvis
28. eating a banana
29. Playing a video game
30. Here is everybody and how they were killed:
    1. Axel - surgical hacksaw to the throat, neck broken.
    2. Nurse Morgan - gutted with a scalpel.
    3. Hitchhiker - knifed through the neck.
    4. Samantha - knifed through a raft.
    5. Paul - speared in the groin.
    6. Terri - speared in the back.
    7. Mrs. Jarvis - killed off screen.
    8. Jimmy - corkscrew through the hand, cleaver in the face.
    9. Tina - thrown through a window, lands on a parked car.
    10. Ted - knifed in the head through a movie screen.
    11. Doug - head crushed in Jason's bare hands.
    12. Sara - axed in the chest.
    13. Rob - garden harrow in the throat.

31. Jason
32. 2 miles, hang right to house.
33. Chris and her parents
34. Axel
35. Scares her
36. Watch the news
37. Wessex County Morgue
38. Jason's
39. Nurse Morgan
40. Nurse Morgan - gutted with a scalpel
41. Axel
42. Axel
43. Mrs. Jarvis and her daughter, Trish
44. Ted and Billy
45. Ted

46.   1930 -1979
47.   Gordan
48.   Red
49.   Sara and Sam
50.   Canada and Love and on the other side it said Fuck You.
51.   knifed through the neck
52.   Sam getting undressed
53.   Sam
54.   Terri and Tina
55.   Crystal Point
56.   Sara
57.   Paul
58.   Tommy and Trish
59.   Sam
60.   Sara
61.   Rob
62.   Bear
63.   You can't be hunting for bear.
64.   To his room
65.   A lot of his things, mask and tricks and etc. (Tommy collected horror stuff and he made masks and stuff).
66.   Tina
67.   Rob's
68.   Trish
69.   Because Paul was dancing with Tina
70.   Sam goes swimming (skinny dipping) in Crystal Lake all by herself and swims out to an inflatable raft and gets killed.
71.   Ted
72.   Ted and Jimmy
73.   Sam
74.   Knifed in the neck, while laying in a inflatable boat.
75.   Goes outside
76.   Jimmy
77.   Ted and then Terri
78.   Paul
79.   Speared in the groin
80.   Rob
81.   It gets ransacked by someone

82. Broken in half
83. He shows her some newspaper articles on Jason Voorhees.
84. Jimmy and Tina
85. Terri
86. Terri
87. Outside on the left-hand corner of the house.
88. Yes
89. When Rob leaves the Jarvis's house it starts thundering in the background, and then it starts again when Tina and Jimmy were in bed and it breaks.
90. The killer
91. Tommy
92. The Jarvis's
93. (6)
94. Rob's tent
95. He scares her
96. Because he thought that she was the killer, Jason
97. Naked ladies/half naked ladies dancing around
98. Doug
99. Jimmy and then Ted
100. The fancy corkscrew
101. Corkscrew through the hand, cleaver in the face.
102. 12 years old
103. Rob
104. Red and black
105. Red
106. Ted
107. Knifed in the head through a movie screen.
108. Light blue
109. White
110. Doug
111. Paul or Ted
112. His bare hands
113. An axe
114. He rips the phone box off the side of the house, disconnecting the phone lines to the Jarvis's house.
115. He knew that danger was near, and he was scared.
116. Next door to the Jarvis's

117. The power went out. (Lights go out)
118. On a wall in the basement.
119. He smashes through an upstairs window to his death.
120. About Jason, Rob had them
121. In the basement
122. A dead body in the bathroom upstairs.
123. Garden harrow in the throat.
124. In the basement next door to the Jarvis family.
125. She hits Jason in the neck with the claw of a hammer, in the hand between ring and middle finger of the left hand and in the left arm and then in the face and knocks the hockey -mask off.
126. An axe
127. Tommy's
128. Trish
129. She was next door, she jumps through a window to get away from Jason.
130. White
131. In the neck with the claw of a claw hammer.
132. Yes
133. A machete
134. After Jason gets stabbed in the side of the face and falls to the floor.
135. The only show him hitting Jason 15 times so it could have been more times.
136. Here are the bloopers:
    1. Part 1 takes place on Friday, June 13th "Present Day". Mrs. Voorhees' tombstone says "Pamela Voorhees 1930 - 1979." But June 13, 1979 isn't a Friday.
    2. In Friday the 13th Part 3, Jason's hands looked like a normal mans, but in Part 4 (which takes place the next day), he has long black fingernails.
    3. When the nurse is mad at Axel, she opens the morgue double doors to leave and Axel holds the right door from closing but the left door stays open as well.
    4. When Trish and her mom are jogging, a bush in front of them moves before they run by it. It looks like the cameraman bushed as he was walking backwards.

5. Rob says when he first meets Tommy and Trish that he is hunting bear, and Tommy says that there are no bears in the area to discredit the story. However, Paul gives a long speech to all the counselors in Part 2 about bear safety, saying that bears are wandering all over the woods even though Part 2 takes place only a few days before Final Chapter.

6. When Paul dances with Tina, she takes his cap and puts it on. A few shots later Paul has it back but he doesn't appear to have taken his arms off her shoulders while he is dancing.

7. When Tina gets thrown out of the window, by Jason you see a top view of the car as she is falling. If you take a look at the car, you can see the car is already dented and the windows are already shattered before she lands.

8. When Terri goes out and moves her bike, we can hear the bike's kickstand being raised. But when Tina looks through the window, both bikes are up and it is doubtful that Jason would have set it back up after killing Terri.

9. When Jimmy is killed you can clearly see that the clever going into his head has got a cut out of it so it will fit his head.

10. When Doug is in the shower, his hair is completely slicked back, but in the shots from outside of the shower you can see through the frosted glass that his hair is "poofy" and hanging over his forehead.

11. When Jason crushes Doug's head in the shower, Jason's mask has two red marks close to his nose. Later in the film, when Tommy and Trish fight Jason, those red marks are no longer there.

12. There's a bench in the second floor hall that is visible when Sara goes from the bathroom to the bedroom to dry her hair on the left wall. However, this same piece of furniture is later seen on the opposite wall in front of the banister railing when Jason chases Trish upstairs.

13. When Sara tries to escape from the house she is unable to open the locked front door. When Rob and Trish go to

investigate, the front door is unlocked, and it doesn't seem like Jason did it.

14. When Trish and Rob go into the house, they look right at the projector screen but don't react to Teddy's blood being all over it.

15. When Jason is trying to get into Tommy's bedroom, the bookcase they use to barricade the door has some toys on it. If you look closely, you will see a yellow and white stuffed animal fall off the second shelf - but in the next shot it is back on the bookcase.

16. When Tommy and Trish hide in Tommy's bedroom, Tommy grabs a chair, which is teetering in his hand then suddenly it is on the floor in the next shot.

17. There is also a purple monster mask hanging from Tommy's ceiling, and when Jason busts through the door, it begins to spin. A few shots later it is hanging still, but in the next shot it is once again spinning.

18. When Gordan (the dog) jumps out the window in one shot he is breaking through glass, but in the next shot he is moving through the window, but there is no glass around him.

19. When Trish jumps out the window you can clearly see that she sinks into the ground (on a mattress of something hidden under the dirt) but when she stands up she is on solid ground.

20. Jason crushes a lamp on the floor and the room becomes pitch dark but a moment later it is lit again by a sudden occurrence of "moonlight".

21. Trish swings the machete at Jason over-handed, but in the next shot she knocks Jason's mask off underhanded.

22. After Jason falls to the floor, and has his head out almost in half, the machete ends up lodged in his face. Right after that, Tommy picks the machete up, and it was just lying flat on the floor.

23. In Friday the 13th Part 3 Jason was stabbed in the leg, but there is no blood stain or cut on his pants in Part 4.

24. Corey Feldman is wearing long, light colored jeans one minute, but when he fights Jason, he is wearing dark cut-off shorts.
25. Tommy shows Rob his mask on a stick and Tommy is shown releasing then holding something like that.
26. Near the start of the movie when Jason is in the morgue: Axel puts his body in the cold box and the door opens back up. Axel goes back to watching the TV and most of the time we can see the door in the back ground but when Jason kills Axel the cold box door has not moved at all.
27. The cover shows Jason's mask but the ax cut is on the wrong side.
28. When the attendants are rolling Jason on a stretcher, his feet are not facing them, but when they come into the room with Axel, it appears that he has switched positions.
29. Jason throws an axe through the door at Sara's head, but when she backs up the axe is firmly stuck in her lower abdomen.
30. When Sara tries to escape from the house she is unable to open the locked front door. When Rob and Trish go to investigate, the front door is unlocked, and it doesn't seem like Jason did it.
31. When Tommy first looks at the machete on the ground, the handle is resting on the corner of the rug, but when he goes to pick it up, it is not on the rug at all.

137. Pink
138 White
139. A tire swing on a rope.
140. A machete
141. Yes
142. Crispin Glover
143. Jimmy
144. Topanga Canyon, California
145. Mass Murderer's body is missing.
146. Ted
147. E. Erich Anderson
148. Ted White
149. Guy sees his girlfriend slain and gets speared in groin.

150. Crystal Point
151. He needed a bypass patch cord.
152. Friday the 13th The Final Chapter
153. Tina and Terri
154. Wessex County Morgue
155. Baby Blue
156. Blue with White trim.
157. It belonged to the kids that rented the house for the weekend.
158. Station wagon
159. Beige and Brown station wagon
160. White
161. Tina's
162. White
163. Pink
164. Pink
165. Flat tires
166. Screw you Pauly
167. Tina's
168. He was trying to climb up the dock and get away from his dead girlfriend and run for his life.
169. A glass of water.
170. (2)
171. Blue
172. Cream
173. Doug and Sara
174. She was trying to open the front door.
175. Baby Blue
176. Dark Brown
177. Brown
178. Camila More and Carey More
179. Arnie Moore and Robert Perault
180. Crispin Glover
181. Corey Feldman
182. Kimberly Beck
183. Joan Freeman
184. Yellow
185. In the barn at Higgin's Haven
186. Kimberly Beck

187. Directed by Joseph Lito
188. Rob - E. Erich Anderson
189. Girl in the shower - Robyn Woods
190. Yes
191. No
192. Looking for the fancy corkscrew and yelling to Ted asking him if he knew where it was.
193. Watching a movie that had naked ladies in it.
194. Cleaning up some broken bottles.
195. Summer and Fall of 1984
196. Yes
197. Jimmy's
198. **62J768**
199. She was standing at the front door trying to open it but it was locked.
200. Looking for Gordan (the dog)
201. A machete
202. The claw of a claw hammer.
203. In the back of the neck.
204. Yellow
205. A screwdriver
206. The trunk
207. No
208. Tina's underwear
209. Tina
210. It was a contest of who could drink a beer the fastest.
211. Navy Blue
212. Baseball cap
213. Paul's
214. You go
215. Take an umbrella.
216. I'm going upstairs.
217. Why? Are you tired?
218. No, do you mind sleeping in the bottom bunk tonight?
219. Why? You want to sleep in the top?
220. No, give me a few minutes, ok? Good night, Teddy Bear.
221. No
222. She said she was going to strangle Tommy.

223. Tangerine
224. Red
225. I think I'm in heaven.
226. I think I'm in love.
227. Yes
228. A kitchen chair.
229. Yes
230. Pink
231. Gray
232. A bottle of wine.
233. A double bladed axe
234. Yes
235. Tommy? You were suppose to leave!! You were suppose to leave!!
236. Yes
237. (2)
238. Tina and Rob
239. A cream or off white window shade.
240. He hit him in the right side of the face where his right eye was.
241. A machete
242. He broke a lamp that was on.
243. Left
244. Right
245. It was stolen.
246. It was not stolen, two people at the hospital are missing, coincidence? Jason is alive.
247. This is a neat room.
248. This is your room?
249. A no, actually it's Paul's room.
250. You're neat.
251. Eating a banana
252. Tina's underwear

Answers to the Friday the 13th (Part V) Trivia Questions

A. Matching:

1.   I
2.   S
3.   H
4.   K
5.   O
6.   Y
7.   M
8.   B
9.   D
10. X
11. Z
12. E
13. A
14. S
15. T
16. F
17. CC
18. P
19. G
20. J
21. R
22. L
23. N
24. V
25. C
26. W
27. Q
28. U
29. BB
30. AA

B. Answer to the following questions about the movie:

31. The paramedics man Roy.
32. Neil and Les
33. Yes
34. They had to get a look at the main man.
35. They both get killed.
36. Pine Hurst
37. Joey
38. Axed to death.
39. Victor J. Fadden
40. Billy
41. Axed in the head.
42. Pam
43. Knifed in Tommy's dream.
44. Ethel
45. Her son Junior.
46. Demon
47. Anita
48. George
49. Matt
50. Sheriff Tucker
51. Because the mayor was upset with the killings and he wanted the person responsible for the killings behind bars.
52. Cal
53. Mayor Cobb
54. Ric Mancini
55. Dominick Brascia
56. Joey was Roy's son.
57. Right hand
58. Because all he did was sit around like some kind of pig or something.
59. Well if that's the way you feel, forget it Vic, just forget it; but, I think you're really out of line.
60. Neil and Les
61. Sheriff Tucker tells Pam near the end of the movie.
62. Near the end of the movie.
63. Impaled on a tractor harrow.

64. A melted chocolate candy bar.
65. Baby blue
66. Baby blue (or ice blue…that is the way I saw them.)
67. The number of ways that the pseudo-Jason was slowed down:
    1. First hit by a bulldozer.
    2. Then cut in arm by chainsaw.
    3. Then the chainsaw was thrown at him.
    4. He is then stabbed in the leg with a pocket knife.
    5. Then hit with a metal pole.
    6. Gets a machete in his arm.
    7. Then falls to his death off of a barn onto metal spikes on ground.

68. Pete
69. Machete in the throat.
70. Marco St. John
71. No
72. Violet and Robin
73. He was trying to start up the car, that Vinnie was supposed to fix.
74. Pine Hurst
75. A bright sunny day, not a cloud in the sky.
76. He is slashed by the pseudo-Jason in the chest.
77. They were doing the laundry, hanging out the laundry to dry.
78. Robin and Violet
79. Juliette Cummins played Robin and Tiffany Helm played Violet.
80. Victor
81. Duke
82. In his ambulance.
83. Reggie and Pam
84. A chainsaw
85. In the shoulder.
86. The chainsaw ran out of gas.
87. Railroad spike through skull into a tree.
88. Pam
89. Richard Young
90. "So that must be the new kid, huh?"

91.   Robin
92.   Tina and Eddie
93.   His eyes
94.   Pseudo Echo
95.   Jake
96.   He was hit in the face with a meat clever.
97.   Jerry Pavlon
98.   Violet
99.   Tina
100.   "I don't think Victor or Joey will be joining us this morning."
101.   Tina
102.   "Or any other morning"
103.   "You don't set a place for a dead person."
104.   Matt
105.   Raymond, a bum, (Who wasn't actually named in the movie; but, I found out on a web site on the web)
106.   "We'll see, Reggie."
107.   He was eating some of his mother's stew.
108.   She was chopping up a chicken, then she grabbed her shot gun.
109.   Spying on Tina and Eddie.
110.   Hunting knife in the stomach.
111.   Tommy's
112.   Jake, Robin and Violet
113.   Reggie and then Pam.
114.   He actually had a lot of things; clothes, a picture of his mom and sister and his dog Gordan, and some Horror masks that he made.
115.   Reggie
116.   Pseudo-Jason
117.   Vinnie
118.   Road flare in the mouth.
119.   In the barn at Pine Hurst.
120.   Neil - machete in Tommy's dream and Les - ice pick in the neck in same dream.
121.   Jason Voorhees
122.   Vinnie and Pete's

123. "I want every inch of this area combed thoroughly bring back anything you find, anything, now get going."
124. What the hell is going on here?
125. You talking to me? I thought you were talking to me, huh sheriff?
126. Sheriff Tucker
127. No it's ok Roy, go ahead get them out of here.
128. Looks like we've got a maniac on the loose, huh sheriff?
129. On a sheet in the Hubbard's woods.
130. Debisue Voorhees
131. Head crushed with a leather strap.
132. John Robert Dixon
133. He was in the Hubbard's woods.
134. Machetied from beneath her bed.
135. In her bed screaming at the sight of Jake's dead body beside her.
136. About to walk down the stairs.
137. Yes
138. Cut scenes:
    1. Robin's machete death is longer with the blood reaching all across her face and neck, the machete goes about 3 - 5 inches higher.
    2. Junior's death was originally shown more graphically. The cleaver was shown slicing thorough his neck, and his head is lopped off.
    3. There was an insert shot of the cleaver in Jake's face. Blood protruded out of it and down his face.
    4. A more graphic scene of Joey's death. His liver and other extremities shot out of his back.
    5. A scene in which Robin and Joey were in a barn. Robin would put a piece of candy in Joey's mouth. Every time that she did this she would give Joey a kiss. It was cut for time restrictions.

139. In the chest.
140. When he falls backwards he cuts himself with the machete that he was holding.
141. Raymond

142. Hunting knife in the stomach.
143. His brother.
144. Demon was a black leather jacket and leather pants.
145. A ring.
146. Pam
147. Well what's up, Pam?
148. A taco, an egg roll and a slice of cheese and sausage pizza
149. Yes
150. "Oh yeah I'll take it."
151. "Get out of town"
152. There wasn't a reason given, but she saw that Tommy had beaten up Junior Hubbard.
153. Stay safe Reckless.
154. They were killed.
155. Anita - throat slashed and Demon - speared through an outhouse wall
156. In the outhouse
157. Miguel A. Nunez, Jr.
158. Jere Fields
159. Riding his motorcycle around his house and hollering to his mom.
160. Decapitated with a cleaver.
161. Ron Sloan
162. Fixing her stew.
163. Cleaver in the head; falls face first into her own stew.
164. Bed
165. A rubber spider on a ring.
166. In the van from the Unger Institute of Mental Health on his way to Pine Hurst.
167. Digging up Jason's body that was in his grave.
168. His granddaddy
169. Headphones and a walkman.
170. Earthworms
171. A machete
172. Unger Institute of Mental Health
173. Pine Hurst Youth Development Center, Private
174. Talking to Victor and trying to give him a chocolate candy bar.

175. Is there someone we should notify?
176. "The mother died while giving birth, I don't know what the hell happened to the father, he took off I guess."
177. Baby blue
178. A bulldozer
179. Reggie darted at the pseudo-Jason, thinking that he was thrown to his death. He was wrong because pseudo-Jason grabbed his ankle and Reggie would have been a goner if Tommy hadn't come conscious and saved the day by hitting the pseudo-Jason in the wrist, causing him to fall off the loft of the barn to his death.
180. Jason Voorhees
181. Reggie's
182. Tommy
183. A machete
184. In the right wrist.
185. The hockey mask
186. A farmer uses it to plow fields and pulls it from behind his tractor.
187. Baby blue
188. A pocket knife
189. It was stormy and rainy
190. When Pam ran out of gas and started walking away from the truck.
191. Violet
192. Matt, George, Anita and Duke.
193. George
194. Pam
195. Jarvis
196. Wahlburg or Walburg? (I found out a very weird and unusual way, even though on some web pages it said Burns)
197. Gotta split there's action.
198. A picture of his mom, sister and dog and some clothes and his horror masks that he made.
199. Pam
200. Tina and Eddie
201. Because they were trespassing on the Hubbard's property.
202. 8 months

203. Junior Hubbard
204. Eddie
205. Matt
206. (3)
207. A clean sheet that needed to be hung out to dry.
208. They found Duke's dead body in the ambulance and then saw the pseudo-Jason and Reggie took off.
209. A cat.
210. A chocolate bar.
211. A chocolate bar.
212. John Shepard
213. It was storming and raining.
214. A flashlight.
215. Pam
216. A knife.
217. Assistant director, Pam Roberts
218. His dog, his sister and his mom.
219. A shotgun.
220. Trying to fix the car engine.
221. Outside of the outhouse.
222. "So what do we have here?"
223. A gardening hoe and a little bag of something, maybe candy or something?
224. Robin
225. Three and half of a one that was melted.
226. Bubble gum
227. Yes
228. Yes
229. Chopping up a chicken.
230. Robin and Joey
231. Victor
232. Right after the woodpile murder.
233. Raymond, Duke, Neil and Les
234. Roy
235. Seeing his son lying there all hacked to bits.
236. He was shocked and surprised.
237. Articles on Jason Voorhees.
238. "What is he like?"

239. "Well he's like any other kid, he's been through a lot, that's all."
240. (11)
241. Male nurse and later you find out that his name is Billy.
242. Pam
243. Road flare in the mouth.
244. He was involved in the movie "Goonies" and couldn't be in it.
245. Garden shears in the eyes.
246. Mark Venturini
247. He said something right after Joey's body was uncovered, on the rated R, he said, "Bunch of Pussies" referring to Robin and Tina and Violet, when Joey's body was uncovered, they screamed and he said on the director's cut and the television version, "Well, I'll be damned."
248. Yes, because the way it was done, if Joey hadn't of gotten killed there wouldn't of been a "pseudo-Jason" running around killing people.
249. He was a good kid.
250. He hugs and kisses Reggie on the forehead.
251. Reggie says "Do me a favor, don't kiss me when there's people around, ok?"
252. "Well, ok, it's cool.
253. She was dancing.
254. Jake says, "I miss Joey already" and Robin says, "So do I" and then Jake says, "I hope that Victor gets what's coming to him."
255. Ethel Hubbard
256. Pete
257. Junior Hubbard
258. Violet
259. Tina
260. "Look, I know how you all feel, this thing is not easy for any of us, so let's just have breakfast."
261. Yes
262. Lana
263. Still inside the restaurant.
264. It was gray with blue doors, (You only see the driver's door)
265. Red

266. Gray
267. Yes
268. A big plate of scrambled eggs.
269. Yes
270. A man standing there with a bloody axe, (she only saw the shoes and the bloody axe that the man was holding.)
271. Yes
272. Yes
273. Beige
274. She got it off the clothesline.
275. Matt's
276. Pam
277. Yes
278. Yes
279. In the left leg.
280. "You hearing me Junior, you talk, you dumb?"
281. A hand holding a meat cleaver.
282. Drugs, some kind of powdery white substance.
283. Kitchen
284. Pink
285. Yes
286. Pete and then Duke.
287. Lana
288. Billy
289. Making Junior's dinner.
290. Her stew.
291. Seasoning, tomatoes, carrots, onions
292. She wanted him to get off his bike and come in and eat her stew.
293. Matt was last seen when Pam and Reggie and Tommy went to see Reggie's brother and then Pam is running through the woods later and finds him dead, so he could of been killed around anytime after Reggie went to see his brother.
294. Junior
295. Because he saw the blue truck and he must have recognized it.
296. Well the last time that you see Duke alive was when he and Roy were at the murder scene of Vinnie and Pete and Roy said

something there, so anytime between after that and before Reggie and Pam find him dead.

297. Caskey Swaim
298. Enchiladas
299. Blue
300. Yes
301. Near a trailer park.
302. Blue
303. No
304. Absolutely no handball playing in the hallway.
305. Lightning
306. She said that she would blow their heads off.
307. Light blue
308. Pink
309. She lost it around the time that she found Matt's dead body as she was running through the woods.
310. Right after they find Duke's dead body.
311. Reggie's
312. "Run Tommy, Run, Run, he'll kill you, listen to me, get out, get out, listen go Tommy run, run please Tommy."
313. Pam
314. Robin
315. He was going to look for Tina and Eddie.
316. Shavar Ross
317. Melaine Kinnamon
318. Tommy is obsessed that Jason is waiting out there, somewhere, even though new he's around 20 and committed to a halfway house in the woods and is apparently plagued by violent dreams of Jason.
319. Jake
320. Sonny Shields
321. He stood at the door and yelled for everyone to come to breakfast.
322. Yo, breakfast!!! Come and get it!!!!
323. Well I could of done that.
324. Good morning, everybody.
325. Call Eddie for breakfast.
326. Fixing Pete and his car.

327. Bloopers:
    1. When Eddie is getting his head crushed by a leather strap. It shows a view behind the tree and the strap is twisting one way. Then it goes back to his head and back behind the tree and it is being twisted the opposite direction.
    2. When Reggie hits "Jason" with the bulldozer there is no blood on the machete then when he is on the ground there is blood on it again.
    3. Jason kills the drug dealers girl friend who works at a restaurant he axes her, the camera shows the axe hitting her horizontally but when she is shown again the axe is stuck in her vertically.
    4. When Pam (Melanie Kinnamon) is running. There is a sweater on her shoulders then there is no sweater, to the sweater on her shoulder many times!
    5. When Anita (Demon's girlfriend played by Jere Fields) is shown after she gets killed her neck moves and she breathes.
    6. When the men are digging up Jason's body in Tommy's dream, the coffin is actually at ground level with dirt piled on it.
    7. Also in Tommy's dream, when Jason holds up his machete he has clean and perfect fingernails when he has been buried in the ground for some time and when he had nasty black fingernails when Tommy met him in Final Chapter.
    8. In the police car that Vic is in there is no screen separating the back of the police car from the front.
    9. Lana smears bright red lipstick on her upper right lip but when she turns to see what made the noise in the diner, it is pressed and perfect looking.
    10. The sound that startles Lana is of breaking plates, but when she finds the cat it's sniffing at some pots on the ground, What actually broke?
    11. When Tina is lying on her back in the woods, a point is made as to how peaceful and quiet it is.
    12. When Tommy, Pam, and Reggie are going to see Demon they pass the same rocks several time.

13. When Demon is talking a dump in the outhouse, his pants are only unzipped but not pulled down.
14. When Demon finds Anita's body, you can see the pulse in her throat.
15. When Ethel is making the stew right before Junior is killed, the level of soup changes depending on whether the shot is in front of her or behind her.
16. When Reggie finds the bodies in Tommy's room Violet is first propped against the wall and then in the second shot she is lying down.
17. When Pam runs through the woods, her sweater magically disappears and reappears in shots later.
18. After Reggie's grandfather flies through the window his head position is one way and then two shots later the head has turned to the left slightly.
19. When Reggie hits Roy with the tractor, the wound/cut appears on his chest only after he has hit the ground. It is most obvious when he is flying back and the headlight from the tractor shows his undamaged suit.
20. When Tommy swings to chop off Roy's arm, you can see that he is not actually holding a machete in his hand.
21. When the cop is explaining to Pam that Roy is the killer, he shows her some newspaper clippings. One of them has a photograph of Jason with his hockey mask on. What brave photographer took that picture?
22. Where did Tommy get that kitchen knife at the end in the hospital? (Explanation - It is also a dream)
23. When the men are digging up Jason's body in Tommy's dream, the coffin is actually at ground level with dirt piled on it. (Explanation - Tommy's unconscious is saying that Jason is not buried far from the surface of his mind.)
24. When the cleaver is pulled from Ethel's head, it is clean.
25. When Violet is stabbed, the machete is pulled out and it is clean.
26. When Tina is lying on her back on the sheet in the woods, a point is made as to how peaceful and quiet it is with birds chirping and the wind blowing. Then when she closes her eyes, Roy approached to kill her and yet there is

not a single twig breaking or a leaf rustling. Roy could not have been that stealthy.

27. The movie Jake and Robin are watching, "A Place In The Sun" does not end with the Montgomery Cliff carrying Shelly Winters off like that. The scene in the boat that they are watching is almost an hour from the end, yet the movie ends right after Jake dies.

328.   Here is everyone and how they were killed:
1. Neil - machete in Tommy's dream.
2. Les - ice pick in the neck in same dream.
3. Joey - hacked up with an axe.
4. Vinnie - road flare in the mouth.
5. Pete - Throat slashed with a machete.
6. Billy - axed in the head.
7. Lana - axed in the chest.
8. Raymond - hunting knife in the stomach.
9. Tina - garden shears in the eyes.
10. Eddie - head crushed with a leather strap.
11. Anita - throat slashed.
12. Demon - speared through an outhouse wall.
13. Junior - decapitated with a cleaver.
14. Ethel - cleaver in the head falls face first into her own stew.
15. Jake - cleaver in the face.
16. Robin - machete from the beneath the bed.
17. Violet - machete in the stomach.
18. Duke - found butchered in his own ambulance.
19. Matt - railroad spike through his head and into a tree.
20. George - eyes gouged out, thrown through a window.
21. Roy - impaled on a tractor harrow.
22. Pam - knifed in Tommy's dream.

329.   "Ma, ma, ma, ma he hurt me ma, you hear me? He hurt me he hurt me ma, will you cut him all up and chop him and kill him? Do you hear me?

330.   Tommy

331.   No

332. Covers him with a blanket and leaves the room and goes upstairs.
333. "What are those nuts up to now?"
334. 92 minutes
335. 1985
336. Frank Mancuso Jr. (Executive) and Timothy Silver
337. Machete
338. (2)
339. Lana - axed in the chest.
340. George - eyes gouged out, thrown through a window.
341. White
342. Corey Feldman
343. Yes
344. Around 20
345. Axed in back of head.
346. 8 years
347. Come on Roy get your hands dirty.
348. Machete
349. When Tommy confronted the pseudo-Jason in the barn, he gives a weird look to Tommy.
350. They were talking to one another as they walked away into the house.
351. She shook the outhouse when Demon was trying to use it.
352. Yes, but a little harder.
353. She was running and slipped and fell in a mud puddle and was trying to get up but she couldn't while being chased by the pseudo-Jason.
354. Machete
355. Reggie
356. Halloween night
357. Machete
358. False or fake
359. Shavar Ross
360. Melanie Kinnamon
361. Rebecca Wood-Sharkey
362. Caskey Swaim
363. They are posters of music bands, like The Alan Parson's Project and The Rolling Stones and some others.

364. Duke
365. Sleeping
366. Severe trauma at age 12, brutal self-defense murder of a psychopathic killer.
367. They've given him every treatment and therapy they can think of. It's a wonder his mind isn't fried from all the drugs they've given him.
368. Pam
369. Looking at a magazine and listening to music and dancing a little.
370. "Can it wait?"
371. No
372. Blue and white striped
373. Jake, I'm sorry, you know sometimes Robin, you are so stupid.
374. Just her underwear.
375. You stay right here, relax and I'll be right back.
376. (11)
377. (22)
378. Reggie and Tommy
379. Yes
380. Richard Lineback, Chuck Wells, Ed Shinstine and Ed Matthews.
381. Dick Wieand
382. Tom Morgan
383. Trailer Park
384. Neon blue
385. Jason Voorhees
386. I said I was sorry.
387. Matt
388. Seeing a dismembered corpse.
389. No
390. Yes
391. Junior
392. A dark blue sweat suit jacket and a baby blue tee-shirt with a pocket in it, the collar was cut off of the tee-shirt and white pants.
393. Gray

394. Yes
395. Hey Matt, how's it going?
396. Alright sheriff, what's up?
397. Well, Matt it's just like we talked about. You got some neighbors that aren't too happy about your place here. Now I certainly know what it is you're trying to do and I respect it Matt, I do. But well you see; we found a couple of your kids on the Hubbard's place again. We found them in the Hubbard's woods. They were screwing their heads off, Matt. Now I think we're all pretty lucky this time because Ethel didn't see them.
398. I'll take care of it, Sheriff.
399. (2)
400. White
401. Yes
402. Yes
403. White
404. Pete
405. A gray rabbit.
406. The car horn.
407. No
408. Some tools, a milk jug, a gasoline can and some other things.
409. Red
410. Stay right here.
411. Stop! Cut it out, don't.
412. No
413. Yes
414. In his room.
415. Yes
416. Left
417. Bright baby blue with a white hood and white top.
418. 8793
419. I'll do the talking and you keep quiet.
420. Lana to go with nothing on her.
421. White
422. (3)
423. (6)
424. Natural wood color with a band of color around them.

425. A green garden hose.
426. Do not write on the walls.
427. Hey Anita, what's up?
428. Joey's
429. Yes
430. Underwear
431. Gray
432. Get up.
433. Yes
434. White
435. Blue jeans
436. In a tool shed in the barn.
437. A horseshoe.
438. "Morning Ethel, my don't you look lovely today."
439. "Horse Shit!" Now Sheriff you better hear me and hear me good I want this loony bin closed down. Do you hear me fella? Now these kids ain't nothing but trouble. They don't respect others property and they're all crazy.
440. Ethel, these kids weren't doing...
441. Doing? Doing? Do you think I don't know what those two perverts were doing in my yard.
442. Junior
443. Tell them like you mean it ma.
444. Would you shut the fuck up?
445. Yes
446. A football.
447. A pile of chopped wood, a croquet set and a green garden hose.
448. Yes
449. Yes
450. Come on.
451. Reggie
452. Pam
453. Pam
454. He pops up on the other side of the Paramedics' ambulance.
455. Reggie
456. Yes
457. Red

458. Gray
459. 1985
460. Tommy's
461. Robin, Jake and Violet
462. Reggie and then Pam
463. He was busy with making the movie "Goonies".
464. His eyes.
465. Pseudo Echo
466. No
467. Right after the first verse of the song.
468. A bloody hand holding a machete.
469. Yes
470. Jason Voorhees
471. Yes
472. Tommy threw a chair or something through the hospital window making it look like he escaped.
473. Yes
474. Ed Shinstine
475. Chuck Wells
476. Suzanne Bateman
477. Yes
478. Vinnie - Anthony Barrile
479. Roy - Dick Wieand
480. Yes
481. Right
482. Olive green T-shirt and army camouflage pants.
483. At breakfast.
484. Pete asked Vinnie.
485. Pete asked Vinnie.
486. Yeah sure, all of those loonies should be killed off one by one.
487. Wooden spoon
488. Wooden bowl
489. Red blanket, socks, boxers.
490. Gray
491. A yellow rain coat.
492. Neil and Les
493. Playboy Magazine
494. Light blue

495.   Yes
496.   Yes
497.   Pushpins and pieces of a paper that was ripped off of it.
498.   Sweater
499.   Red
500.   Get lost!
501.   Come on don't be like that I came to help you with the wood today and I have two candy bars, see? Don't tell the girls.
502.   Gees, what an asshole.
503.   Blue
504.   Yes
505.   White
506.   Light green shirt, when he is found dead.
507.   A dirty white shirt with a hole in it.
508.   A dark blue short sleeve T-shirt with white bands around the sleeves and a white #10 on the back.
509.   A red plaid shirt that had dark blue and white on it.
510.   Gray
511.   Tina
512.   A pond nearby.
513.   Yes
514.   He recognized the blue pickup truck.
515.   (2)
516.   Reggie and Tommy
517.   Roy and Billy
518.   Machete
519.   Gray but it's dirty looking.
520.   A melted chocolate candy bar.
521.   Danny Steinmann
522.   Because he was dead and buried.
523.   Red sweat suit.
524.   Trips and falls.
525.   The real Jason's hockey mask has a brig red triangle on it and a cut in the left side where Chris hit him in the head in Part 3 and the pseudo-Jason's has two blue triangles on it.
526.   Olive green
527.   Red with a white top.
528.   Executive Producer - Frank Mancuso Jr.

529. (3)
530. Jason Voorhees
531. You are out of your fucking mind, you've been out in the sun to long; Jason Voorhees is dead. His body was cremated. He's nothing but a handful of ash.
532. (2)
533. Your ass is on the line here Tucker, are you getting that? You get me a live suspect.
534. Threw his ashtray at the board next to the door that keys were hanging on.
535. Sheriff's office.
536. He took off somewhere I guess.
537. (1)
538. Seeing a dismembered corpse.
539. (4)
540. Late summer to early fall 1984.
541. Directed by Danny Steinmann
542. A couple of days.
543. (1)
544. (1)
545. (4)
546. (3)
547. You know that for sure mayor? Were you there?
548. Red
549. Red
550. (1)
551. (2)
552. (4)
553. Neon blue
554. Reggie, Pam and Tommy
555. White with black trim.
556. Black
557. Piss off
558. Well if that's the way you feel I'll go help somebody else instead; but if you change your mind I'll be right around.
559. They yelled his name in an annoyed tone.
560. A Place In The Sun
561. I really want to make love with you.
562. A red bag.

Answers to Friday the 13th (Part 6) Trivia Questions:

A. Matching:

1. F
2. V
3. K
4. A
5. J
6. B
7. C
8. D
9. E
10. G
11. H
12. I
13. L
14. M
16. N
17. O
18. U
19. P
20. S
21. R
22. T

B. Questions: Answers to the questions:

23. Allen Hawes
24. He gets killed by Jason
25. Heart ripped out.
26. Broken bottle in the throat.
27. The cemetery caretaker.
28. He dug up Jason's body.
29. Lightning strikes him.
30. Lake Forest Green

31. The sheriff said that he wanted the people to forget about all that had happened there.
32. Tommy
33. At the bottom of Crystal Lake.
34. C. J. Graham
35. Well Tommy dug Jason up and stabbed Jason with a metal pole and then lightning hit Jason and brought him back to life.
36. Cremate him.
37. In the back of the cemetery.
38. He was buried when Tommy was 12.
39. Maggots and cobwebs and worms.
40. It starts when Tommy tries to light a match, after Jason is brought back from the dead.
41. Fuck you, Jason.
42. Jason's hockey mask.
43. Tommy lets go, I don't think my heart can take anymore of this.
44. He gets killed, Jason rips his heart out and Allen lands in Jason's coffin and the top of it closes on him.
45. He runs to his pickup truck to go for help.
46. The sheriff's office.
47. No, not until he goes out to the camp and faces Jason.
48. Lizabeth and Darren
49. Darren - impaled on a spear and tossed aside.
50. Lizabeth - speared through the mouth.
51. Her money and credit cards.
52. Megan
53. Yes, a little while before the end of the movie, he does go there.
54. A number of things: can goods, vegetables, popcorn, ketchup, mustard, toilet paper
55. Friday the 13th
56. Sissy
57. They are playing a game and she tags them, they are playing paint ball or gotcha.
58. Burt was very upset.
59. Jason's bare hands.
60. Yes

61. Roy
62. The cemetery, to Jason's grave.
63. Martin
64. Yes
65. One of the deputies.
66. No
67. In the woods.
68. Steven and Annette
69. Nancy
70. Jason
71. Nikki's step-father
72. Cort
73. Jason
74. Teenage Frankenstein
75. Alice Cooper
76. Nikki
77. In the bathroom of the motor home.
78. Knife rammed through the skull.
79. It flips on to it's side and moves a little ways and then it is on fire.
80. Red
81. Occult
82. One machete rips through two people on a motorcycle.
83. Steven and Annette's
84. Tommy
85. Karloff's General something?
86. Half an hour
87. Roy's
88. Cuts the phone line.
89. Sissy
90. Baker
91. Sissy
92. Tommy
93. A Camero.
94. He's Back, The Man Behind the Mask
95. Sissy's
96. Her father's deputies.
97. Megan

98. A troublemaker.
99. Rick
100. Paula
101. Paula
102. Rick
103. His revolver that has a laser scope.
104. He gets locked up in the jail cell that Tommy was in.
105. Tommy's plan at first was to dig him up and cremate his body and then the last plan was to get him to his final resting place in Crystal Lake.
106. Two car doors slam and Jason hears it, it was the Sheriff and his Deputies.
107. Officer Thorton.
108. Dart in the forehead.
109. Jason
110. She wasn't in bed, she was outside trying to convince the deputies that a monster was out there.
111. The order was to lie down on the floor under their beds and not to move until he returned.
112. He finds him behind one of the cabins.
113. He tries using a revolver with blanks.
114. A dead person, Officer Thorton.
115. A big heavy chain.
116. A very big rock.
117. A decapitated head, Sissy's.
118. Yes
119. He was killed by Jason.
120. Maggot head, Asshole, Chicken Shit, Pussy
121. He calls him those names to get him angry at Tommy so that he would come after Tommy.
122. Yes, but then Jason disappears from view under the lake.
123. Gasoline
124. No, he drowned.
125. She swims over to rescue Tommy, then she gets her leg grabbed by Jason and pulled under, until she gets the boat motor and starts it up and turns it towards Jason and it takes care of Jason.
126. The boat motor propeller.

127.   It's finally over, it's finally over, Jason is home.
128.   No, but for now he is gone.
129.   Bloopers:
     1. In Part V the cop says that Jason Voorhees was cremated, yet Tommy digs up Jason's grave. (Explanation - Either the cop was mistaken or (more likely) he was lying to dispel rumors.)
     2. When Tommy is stabbing Jason with the fence post, the corpse shakes and seems hollow and dried out - yet when he is resurrected he sure seems meaty.
     3. In the coffin, a maggot falls straight "down" off of Jason's face even though he is supposedly lying down.
     4. The truck that Tommy jumps into to escape Jason revs up before he has a chance to start it.
     5. After Cort and Lizabeth bring their groceries from the truck you can see their reflection in the side panel of the truck as they walk past the camera and then sit down and wait for the scene to end.
     6. When Jason chops off the three survivalist's heads and the corpses fall down, you can see the mat on the ground onto which they fall.
     7. When Tommy makes a sharp turn for the graveyard and the sheriff says, "Hit the noise and the cherries!" Inside the police car it is shown going straight; but, the shot before showed the car right on Tommy's tail, which means they should be turning - which they do in the subsequent shot.
     8. In the motor home, Cort's shirt starts out rolled up tight almost to his chin but in subsequent shots it rolls down without Cort or Nikki touching it.
     9. When Cort is driving the motor home everything inside the motor home is moving back and forth. There is a framed picture behind Cort that is moving back and forth. Once Jason grabs Nikki and pulls her into the bathroom the frame stops moving, but after Jason kills her and right before he kills Cort you can clearly see in the background the framed picture moving back and forth again.
     10. In the motor home, Cort turns up the Alice Cooper song, but the volume remains the same.

11. When Sissy pours the soda out the window you can see something in the bottom left of the window (most likely the camera used to shoot the reverse angle.)

12. During the police chase scene officer Papas reports Megan's license plate number to the sheriff even though she is driving backwards and there is no plate on the front.

13. During both the police chase scene and the scene where Jason stops the counselors in the middle of the road there are scenes of nighttime, daylight, and nighttime again in the same scene.

14. After Jason chops the caretaker with the machete, he sees Steven and starts walking after him. His machete disappears in a side shot of him walking through the woods.

15. The little girl is holding Jason's machete, carrying it into Paula's cabin. When the little girl is walking with the machete outside, the machete has some blood on it, but when she hands the machete to Paula it is covered with blood. Also the front end of the machete is pointed directly towards Paula, but when Paula gets startled it shows the little girl holding it with the front end pointing up.

16. When Tommy and Megan are driving in the woods towards the camp near the end of the film, they reuse a shot from the earlier police chase - you can see the red police lights reflected on the trees.

17. In the beginning when they have the close up of Jason's eye (in the James Bond spoof) it is brown, but at the end when Megan cuts his neck with the propeller, his eye is blue, and then it is brown again for the last shot of Jason.

18. When Jason gets the propeller in the face, it hits his left cheek, but 5 seconds later, it turns out a chunk is missing from the right side of his mask and then on Part 7, the chunk is missing on the left side again.

19. The propeller's damage to Jason changes from shot to shot.

20. Jason's pants are pinched cuffed at the bottom near his ankles you see that during the scene when they show his legs walking fast in the woods. Then you notice that they

are not pinched cuffed anymore in the part when he charges into the cabin and all the kids go back under the bed.

21. When Jason stabs Cort in the head, in the front view you can see the knife shaking like rubber.

22. On the back of the box the word Voorhees is spelled wrong, it is spelled Vorhees.

23. When Jason crushed the cop's head his sides of his head were pushed in but when Jason lets go of him his head went back to its normal place.

24. When Jason rips out Allen's heart he puts his hand in his stomach. Your heart is located to the left of your chest.

25. Jason gets a belt from that guy playing paintball Burt, but Jason has it in Part 7.

26. The first time that Tommy Jarvis is put in the jail cell, the policeman shuts the door but fails to lock the cell. It shows later that they key does lock the cell when Tommy throws that same policeman there.

27. When the group of kids enter the police station, Cort has his headphones down around his neck. In the next shot, the sheriff asks him if "his parents have a sewing machine,"

28. When Jason kills Lizabeth, the first shot shows Jason with his feet on either side of her head, but in the next shot, his feet are together.

29. After Cort and Paula bring their groceries from the truck you can see their reflection in the side panel of the truck as they walk past the camera and then sit down and wait for the scene to end.

30. When Jason kills Burt, the first survivalist, he presumably takes Burt's weapons and belt, yet Jason is wearing the belt when he lifts Burt's arm right after killing him.

31. When Jason chops off the three survivalist's heads and the corpses fall down, you can see the mat on the ground onto which they fall.

32. When Cort starts up the motor home, all the lights come on, but after Jason has killed Nikki and stabbed Cort, you

can see that it is completely dark inside (look right before it tips over.)

33. After Jason chops the caretaker with the machete, he sees Steven and starts walking after him. His machete disappears in a side shot of him walking through the woods.

34. The front end of the machete is pointed directly towards Paula, but when Paula gets startled it shows the little girl holding it with the front end pointing up.

35. When the sheriff shoots Jason with the shotgun the first time, the black cable, which pulls Jason back is clearly visible to the left of the screen.

36. When Tommy pours gasoline onto the lake, he splashes it in two lines along the sides of his boat, yet when he throws a match onto the gasoline it manages to ignite in a nice circle around him.

37. Jason grabs Megan's ankle, and has to reach up from being held down by the rock. But when Megan reaches the boat motor, how is she able to cut his head and neck when he is supposedly more than 5 or 6 feet below the water?

38. The propeller's damage to Jason changes from shot to shot.

39. In many shots of the lake from the shore, the water is always murky and brown, but in the shots taken from underwater when Jason and Tommy are fighting, the water is very clear and blue.

130. Here are all the characters and how they were killed:
1. Allen - heart ripped out.
2. Darren - impaled on a spear and tossed aside.
3. Lizabeth - speared through the mouth.
4. Burt - arm ripped off and impaled on a tree branch.
5., 6., 7. Stan and Katie and Larry - tripled decapitation with a machete.
8. Martin - broken bottle in the throat.
9., 10. Steven and Annette - double impaled with a machete on their motorcycle.
11. Nikki - face crushed against RV wall.

12. Cort - hunting knife in the head.
13. Roy - pieces of him found strewn in the woods.
14. Sissy - head ripped off.
15. Paula - hacked up with a machete.
16. Officer Thornton - dart in the forehead.
17. Officer Pappas - head crushed in Jason's bare hands.
18. Sheriff Garris - broken in half.

131.　Yes

132.　(1.) Tommy's side kick, Allen's insides were ripped out of his body, not just a hand through his chest. Jason dragged the guts out and dropped them on the ground where it lays steaming (his heart.)

2.　The bottle-in-the-neck death of the caretaker was cut to shreds. The X-rated version of that had Jason ramming the broken bottle in to his neck. He goes down and the camera closes in as the blood begins to ooze out of one end.

3.　The triple decapitation of goofy survivalists was cut too. It showed their heads sliced right off.

4.　The two camp counselor's deaths on the road were also cut.
    a. The woman speared in the water was cut of excess blood.
    b. The man was speared, lifted into the air and slid down the spear leaving his insides on the spear.

5.　Cort's death was cut a lot too. He was stabbed in the side of the head and blood began to pour out.

6.　The wall to wall blood cabin was also cut. There were shots of livers and hearts running down the walls but it was cut out.

7.　Sissy's death was toned down. In the uncut version you could see her head torn clean off and dropped.

8.　The backbreaking sheriff's scene was also cut. There were more screams, bones crushing, and his legs began kicking.

9.　A scene after Allen gets thrown in Jason's coffin where Jason's father Elias (red haired) walks over his grave and senses that he is not there.

133.　Jason

134. A chain with a huge rock at the end of the chain.
135. Tommy
136. Yes
137. Red (but they call it orange)
138. Baby blue
139. Tommy
140. Jason is brought back to life and he opened his eyes.
141. Two and the kids from the summer camp.
142. (18)
143. Jason
144. Megan
145. Yes
146. Cort
147. Nikki's step-father, Horace
148. Cort
149. A shovel
150. In the back of the head
151. A crowbar
152. He must have really messed you over.
153. Nancy
154. Yes
155. Nancy
156. One of his deputies.
157. He lights a match and throws it where he poured the gasoline.
158. Annette and Steven's
159. Covington, GA
160. Tom McLoughlin
161. Don Behrns
162. Harry Manfredini
163. 1986
164. 87 minutes
165. Michael Nomad
166. Teenage Frankenstein, He's Back The Man Behind the Mask
167. Leeches
168. Martin Becker
169. June 13th, 1986
170. Tyen
171. Billy

172. So what were you going to be when you grew up?
173. Broken in half.
174. Yes
175. Nancy
176. Lizabeth
177. Speared through the mouth.
178. Paramount Pictures
179. 25 million
180. Yes
181. Tom Matthews, Jennifer Cooke and CJ Graham as Jason
182. Megan
183. Renee Jones
184. It was a lot of fun, even though he wasn't into acting.
185. Ron Palillo
186. Allen
187. Heart ripped out.
188. Kerry Noonan
189. Yes
190. Hawes and when he gets killed, Horace.
191. Yes
192. Yes
193. No
194. Tommy's friend Allen
195. Yes
196. Yes
197. Yes
198. The Head Counselors
199. His mail order laser scope that is on his revolver.
200. If this is as exciting as it gets we are in big trouble dude.
201. A ring.
202. Because the first guy did not have the power that the director wanted.
203. Yes
204. Yes
205. Yes
206. Thom Matthews
207. Jennifer Cooke
208. Eternal Peace Cemetery

209. As a child, Tommy Jarvis did what many others died trying to do. He killed Jason Voorhees, the mass murder who terrorized the residents of Crystal Lake. But now, years later, Tommy is tormented by the fear that maybe Jason isn't really dead. So Tommy and a friend go to the cemetery to dig up Jason's grave. Unfortunately, for Tommy, (and ever unfortunately for his friend), instead of finding a rotten corpse, they discover a well rested Jason who comes back from the dead for another bloody rampage in Friday, the 13th Part VI: Jason Lives.
210. Yes
211. Brown
212. A tall man in a dark suit, with a thin pale face that was framed by long dark red hair streaked with gray. It showed not a flicker of expression. The features were fine and chiseled, deeply etched. The mouth was thin and cruel. But the eyes, don't look at them eyes, the eyes were like a snake's eyes, cold, feral and ancient.
213. A metal pole off the cemetery fence.
214. January of 1986.

Answers for the Friday the 13th (Part 7): The New Blood Trivia Questions:

A. Matching:

1.   H
2.   Q
3.   R
4.   I
5.   K
6.   B
7.   E
8.   C
9.   G
10.   D
11.   F
12.   J
13.   O
14.   L
15.   N
16.   M
17.   P
18.   T
19.   A
20.   S

B. Questions:

21.   Kane Hodder
22.   Telekinesis
23.   Using telekinesis, Tina summons her dead father to pull Jason back into the depths of Crystal Lake.
24.   Tina
25.   He drowned in Crystal Lake when Tina was little.
26.   Friday, October 13.
27.   Nick

28. Buzz saw 2000 saw in the stomach.
29. Melissa
30. (2)
31. Dr. Crews
32. To get it to move.
33. There's a legend 'round here, a killer buried but not dead. A curse on Crystal Lake, a death curse, Jason Voorhees curse, they say he died as a boy, and he keeps coming back, few have seen him and lived, some have even tried to stop him no one can (they show the scene from Part 6 of Tommy and Jason's fight. Then after Jason is under the water.) People forget, he's down there waiting.
34. She tried to bring her dead father back.
35. Jason Voorhees
36. Jason Voorhees, (a man)
37. Fainted
38. A metal tent spike
39. Michael
40. Metal tent spike in his back.
41. Tent spike in the neck and impaled on a tree.
42. Jane
43. Nick was Michael's cousin
44. Judy
45. Bashed against a tree in her sleeping bag.
46. Jason's hand through his body, neck broken.
47. Machete
48. Michael
49. Speared from behind.
50. Amanda Shepherd
51. Picked on her and thought it was funny.
52. Tina broke Melissa's pearl necklace that her father gave her for being the best daughter.
53. Axed in face.
54. Pulled under Crystal Lake and drowned.
55. Bloopers:
    1. Judy, the girl in the sleeping bag is about to be killed. Jason picks it up at the end where her head is. He then carries it to the tree and smacks the opposite end against it. That

would be her feet and legs, but, when the bag falls open, her head is all mangled and bloody.

2. At the end of Part 6, Jason has the gloves on when he is underwater. But in Part 7 it shows the parts from the last movie, you see him with the gloves on, then with the gloves off.

3. Jason's clothes are torn to shreds. Then in Part 8 they are fine.

4. Also in Part 7, when Jason kills robin he throws her out the window with her back to it, but when it shows the shot from outside she is thrown out face first.

5. Right before Jason kills the stoned guy in the kitchen he calls out the name Maddy when the one he was sleeping with was named Robin.

6. At the end of Part 7 Jason isn't wearing gloves, but when he is brought back to life he is wearing gloves.

56. Cut scenes:

1. David, the stoner's death is longer. He gets stabbed in the stomach and is thrown head first into the water faucet, cracking his head open.

2. Dr. Crews' death scene was trimmed substantially. Originally, there was a shot of the blade of the "Bushmaster 2000" (the weed/eater-looking thing.) Cutting into the doc's stomach. The guts inside sucked the blade in sending guts flying through the air.

3. A reaction shot was trimmed from Melissa's death. Originally, there was a quick cut of the axe slamming into her face, but that was cut after the MPAA saw it.

4. The head crushing of Ben was cut severely. If you look really closely at the released cut, you can see the blood start to squirt. Originally, that was much longer and his head crushes in.

5. Russ's death was cut as well. In the uncut version, the guy's face splits open as the axe slams into it. The folks on the set referred to this as the "Cootchie-face" effect.

6. The dude gathering firewood. There was a shot of Jason's hand ripping through the front of his body, but that was cut.
7. The death of Eddie was cut severely. In the cut version, you hear his head drop to the floor. Originally, that was shown.

57. Here is everyone and how they were killed:
    1. John Shepherd - drowned in Crystal Lake.
    2. Jane - tent spike in the neck, impaled on tree.
    3. Michael - tent spike in his back.
    4. Dan - Jason's hand through his body, neck broken.
    5. Judy - bashed against a tree in her sleeping bag.
    6. Russell - axed in the face.
    7. Sandra - pulled underwater and drowned.
    8. Maddy - scythed in the neck.
    9. Ben - head crushed in Jason's bare hands.
    10. Kate - party horn in the eye.
    11. David - butcher knife in the stomach.
    12. Eddie - beheaded with a machete.
    13. Robin - thrown through a window.
    14. Amanda Shepherd - speared from behind.
    15. Dr. Crews - Buzzsaw 2000 saw in the stomach.
    16. Melissa - axed in face.

58. Tina uses her mental powers to pull tree roots out of the ground and wrap around Jason's legs and pull him into a muddy puddle of water and then she pulled down an electric telephone line and electrocutes Jason. She runs to the kids' house next door, and slams the door. After Jason smashes through a window; she uses her mental powers and blocks the door with a table and shuts the door and then throws the couch on Jason. She then throws the potted plant that has the decapitated head of someone, in it and runs out of the front door, and then she uses her powers again to make the roof crash down on Jason and then she breaks a light in his hockey mask covered face and it makes him crash through the stairs, and then she uses her mental powers and squeezes his mask so

hard in the back that puss starts oozing out and then breaks his hockey mask in two when he turns around and then strangles him with a electrical light cord and then breaks the floor and drops him into the basement, she then throws nails at him and then pours gasoline all over him and everything in the basement and then, setting him on fire from the furnace and then the house blows up and then finally calling her dead father to pull Jason back in to the depths of Crystal Lake.

59. Telekinesis
60. Michael's
61. A metal tent spike.
62. Blood
63. A cat.
64. Because he was with Tina's mom when she got killed.
65. Nick and Tina
66. (16)
67. It blew up.
68. She saw her mother being killed by Jason, in front of her in the road in a delusion.
69. Nighttime
70. Left
71. He was crushing Nick's spine with his foot.
72. One time they look pink, and another time they look blue the eyeball is yellow.
73. A broken chain from Part 6, that had held him down under the lake.
74. Jason's hockey mask that is broken in half.
75. Nick and Tina
76. Doctor Crews
77. She screams
78. No
79. (7)
80. Fire and gasoline.
81. Jason Voorhees
82. 1988
83. 90 minutes
84. (9)
85. She gets scared and shakes and then the whole room shakes.

86. Lar Park Lincoln
87. Kevin Blair
88. Susan Blu
89. Deep breathing
90. Terry Kiser
91. Yes
92. He was arguing with her mom and he supposedly hit her mom.
93. She is in a motor boat in the lake.
94. "I hate you, I wish you were dead."
95. Yes
96. Yes
97. Yes
98. A party favor gouged into an eye
99. Kate's
100. Car trouble
101. (5)
102. It explodes.
103. Night
104. October 13th
105. Young Tina, her mom and dad.
106. Bad character, you find out near the end.
107. Nick
108. Dr. Crews
109. When she is upset.
110. Night
111. A radio and a burgundy duffel bag.
112. Jane's dead body.
113. No
114. David
115. David
116. Dan
117. He heard a noise behind him.
118. "Dan is that you? Come and get me you big hunk of a man."
119. Yes
120. Melissa
121. Sandra was skinny dipping in Crystal Lake and Russell was getting undressed to join her.
122. Eddie

123.   A metal spike and a videotape.
124.   Silver gray
125.   Butcher knife in the stomach.
126.   Maddy
127.   Scythed in the neck.
128.   In the tool shed.
129.   Scythe
130.   Because he thinks Michael is out there and he wanted to surprise him.
131.   Michael
132.   Having sex
133.   To get something to eat.
134.   He was hungry.
135.   White
136.   Pink, orange and lt. blue.
137.   Red
138.   Mud
139.   Yes
140.   Looking in the refrigerator for something to eat.
141.   In a desk drawer
142.   Tina found some old newspaper articles and realizes who the man in the lake that she brought back is.
143.   A magnifying glass (called a personal penis enlarger).
144.   Light blue
145.   David's
146.   Robin
147.   Dark tabby
148.   No
149.   Bare hands
150.   Melissa
151.   Yes
152.   Buzz saw 2000 saw
153.   In the woods
154.   Yes
155.   Pink and blue
156.   Back over next door to bed.
157.   Yes
158.   A piece of her jacket.

159.   Yes, for now he is gone until the next movie.
160.   An earring
161.   Axed in the face.
162.   Robin
163.   David
164.   Metal tent spike
165.   Her father.
166.   For being the best daughter.
167.   Eddie
168.   Robin
169.   (15)
170.   Michael
171.   Yes
172.   Pink and gold
173.   Michael's
174.   His girlfriend, Jane
175.   David
176.   Yes
177.   Baldwin County, Alabama
178.   John Carl Buechler
179.   Frank Mancuso Jr. (Executive), Tain Paterson and Barbara Sachs (Associate)
180.   Michael's
181.   Kane Hodder
182.   Because he got killed by Jason.
183.   Pittsburgh
184.   Yes
185.   I'll be back.
186.   1988
187.   35,000,000
188.   20,000,000
189.   Paramount Pictures
190.   (9)
191.   Yes
192.   Tina
193.   Maddy's
194.   His cousin Michael
195.   Lar Park Lincoln, Susan Blu and Terry Kiser

196.   She once touched the head in the flowerpot and then went "crazy".
197.   Sandra and Melissa
198.   Melissa
199.   Russell
200.   His cousin Michael
201.   Yes
202.   Baby blue
203.   White
204.   Yes
205.   Maddy
206.   8 weeks
207.   5 miles
208.   Mud
209.   What the fuck.
210.   Jason
211.   6' 7"
212.   2 to 3 hours

Answers For Friday the 13th (Part 8) Trivia Questions:

A. Matching:
1.   J
2.   H
3.   U
4.   S
5.   R
6.   O
7.   E
8.   Q
9.   P
10.   C
11.   D
12.   F
13.   K
14.   L
15.   M
16.   N
17.   G
18.   I
19.   W
20.   A
21.   B
22.   Y
23.   T
24.   V
25.   X

B. Answer to the Questions:

26.   On a ship.
27.   In Manhattan
28.   Sanitation Worker
29.   Kane Hodder
30.   A dog

31.   Yes
32.   On a small boat, around the vicinity of Camp Crystal Lake.
33.   Jim and Suzi
34.   A boat anchor dragging across the bottom of the lake, hits the cable that Jason is lying near and shakes it up and down and sparks and smoke fly from it, and Jason gets electrocuted and is brought back to life.
35.   Yes
36.   Pretending to be Jason and stab her with a fake knife.
37.   She was hiding in a storage area of the small boat.
38.   Stabbed with a spear in the chest.
39.   30 years
40.   Her English teacher
41.   A pen that Stephen King supposedly used in high school.
42.   The pen that was her gift from Collen Van Deusen.
43.   Lakeview High
44.   The 13th.
45.   A rope hanging from the side of the ship.
46.   Admiral Robertson
47.   Bloopers:
   1.   When Rennie is at her sink, and the little boy Jason is appearing in the glass to strangle her, she has her hands covered with blood. But, in the next scene when she's on the floor we see clearly her right hand and it is clean.
   2.   Rennie and Sean open the door and water rushes out, the water is sort of green in the beginning.
   3.   In Part 7 Jason had a right eye but no left eye. In Part 8 he had a left eye but no right eye.
   4.   When they are in the police car everyone is in the back seat. But when Rennie drives the car in to the wall Sean gets out of the front seat.
   5.   When Rennie throws the barrel of toxic waste on Jason how does the toxic waste get there if the sewer floods out every night at midnight?
   6.   While everyone that is left is boarding the escape raft, Jason is standing up on deck and a sprinkler is noticeable above him, which is supposedly giving off the rain for the scene, check it out.

7. The captain of the ship gets his throat slashed, but no blood gushes out, and if you watch closely, the machete barely makes contact with his throat.

8. Jason is a bald little child, yet in the narrative flashback, Jason's appearance as child has changed drastically, making him normal.

9. Julius runs to a pay phone to call the police and dials 9-1-1, but then he says, "Operator, this is an emergency, give me the police!"

10. Jim has an exact replica of Jason's mask (destroyed in Part 7) right down to the axe cut from Part 3.

11. In Part 7 Jason's clothes were shredded and you could see his spine, kneecaps, etc. But now his clothes appear intact. Also, he's got a nice new pair of black gloves.

12. In the extreme close-up of Jason's hands grabbing onto the boat's railing you can see Kane Hodder's very human looking pinky finger sticking out of the glove.

13. When JJ is below deck jammin' she is playing her guitar along with a tape in her boom box, but right after she drops her guitar to run, the music stops playing too.

14. When Jason attacks the white boxer in the sauna he rams the hot coal into his stomach right above his belly button. However, in the overhead shot, the coal is jammed into the middle of his chest.

15. When Jason throws Wayne into the electrical switchboard, Wayne's jeans light on fire before he hits the board (check in slow motion). A small spark causes the combustion, and you can see that his pants were obviously soaked with some flammable liquid.

16. Jason teleports up the ship mast to throw off Miles. Sure it's intentional, but it's still stupid.

17. Also, Rennie stabs Jason in the left eye, but later when Jason takes off his mask his left eye hasn't been touched, even though Jason had no left eye but a right eye in Part 7.

18. When Tamara comes out of the shower, she's completely dry - hair and all.

19. When Jason punches off Julius' head, it detaches with a clean, straight line.

20. The wall that Sean emerges from after Rennie was injected with drugs, is obviously a set because you can see the wooden props holding the wall up behind him through the doorway.

21. How did Jason know that the Uncle would run into that building and come up to the second story? And how did Jason get there so fast? (Yes, again it's intentional, and stupid.)

22. When everyone is in the police car, there is no barrier between the front and back seats something is there in an NYPD cruiser.

23. When the police car hits the wall and explodes you can tell that there are just dummies in the back by the way they bob back and forth.

24. When they are in the police car everyone is in the back seat. But when Rennie drives the car into the wall, Sean gets out of the front seat from a seated position.

25. Rennie says she was attacked by Jason as a child when she was learning to swim in Crystal Lake. How is this possible, if the first movie supposedly takes place long before Rennie would be old enough to go swimming, and Jason came out of the lake anywise after Part 1, so he wouldn't have been there when Rennie went swimming.

26. Sewer tunnel entrances in Manhattan are barricaded to prevent people from going down there.

27. There is a shot of Sean and Rennie on the ladder trying to escape the sewer where Rennie is almost.

28. In Part 7 Jason's left eye was bad. In Part 8 his right eye is bad.

29. Jason is a bald little child, yet in the narrative flashback, Jason's appearance as a child has changed drastically, making him normal.

30. When the anchor catches on the electric line, the water is crystal clear, blue and it appears to be lighted, when it is supposed to be dark out.

31. In the scene when Sean and Rennie are talking on the boat, he reaches into his pocket and tries to take out the bracelet, but then in the next shot Rennie already has it in her hand.

32. Also when JJ is down there, the first shot of Jason coming down the stairs ends with his left foot coming down, but in the next shot, it's his right foot coming down.
33. When JJ gets whacked with her own guitar, her blood clearly splatters on a piece of glass in front of the camera just before Jason hits her.
34. When the crazy deckhand appeared after the captain was killed, he said that Jason Voorhees was on the ship. The uncle said that they had been spouting about Jason ever since he came aboard, even though all he said was that the "voyage was doomed", and had not mentioned Jason before then.
35. When Tamara and Eva are doing drugs, their hair keeps changing from shot to shot, from behind their shoulders to in front of their shoulders.
36. When Tamara pushes Rennie overboard, the ship is not moving otherwise it would have left her far behind. Also, the water is calm with no waves from the boat.
37. Jason teleports up the ship mast to throw off Miles. Sure it's intentional, but it's still stupid.
38. When Jason punches off Julius' head, it detaches with a clean, straight line.
39. When the cop gets pulled from his car, by Jason they are in an alley right next to the car. But in the next shot, Jason is standing a good 20 feet away right in front of the car. Why would he have done that instead of just reaching in and killing everyone else?
48. A sexton, that he used when he was his son's age and a computer one.
49. The deck hand.
50. Lazarus
51. A necklace that had a pendant on it of the Statue of Liberty.
52. Wayne
53. Wayne
54. JJ and then later Wayne.
55. When Tamara takes her shower.
56. Hot sauna rock in the chest.
57. She pushes Rennie overboard.

58. Sean
59. Charles McCullough
60. Stabbed with a mirror shard.
61. Harpooned in the back.
62. Jason kills him.
63. Throat slit with a machete.
64. Yes
65. Her uncle who was Charles McCullough
66. Eva
67. She was strangled.
68. A crewmember.
69. Julius, Wayne, Miles
70. Julius
71. The engine room.
72. A shotgun.
73. Electrocuted on a control panel.
74. JJ's dead body.
75. Wayne was electrocuted that is the reason that it catches on fire.
76. He lost his glasses.
77. The fire alarm.
78. Julius
79. Miles
80. Julius
81. Jason
82. The engine room.
83. In the restaurant.
84. The deck hand.
85. Engine room.
86. Collen Van Deusen
87. She is Rennie's English teacher.
88. Axed in the back.
89. The mast.
90. Jason
91. Julius
92. No, they say he drowned as a boy.
93. (6)
94. (7)

95.   Julius
96.   He knows this because he sees the Statue of Liberty.
97.   Charles and Julius
98.   Shaped like a rowboat.
99.   Sean, Rennie, and Collen
100. New York, New York
101. They rob them and shoot at Rennie's dog and kidnap Rennie.
102. Jason
103. Rennie
104. Rennie's dog Toby.
105. Julius
106. Princess
107. #1 - Stabbed through the back with his own syringe and #2 - bashed and scalded on a steam pipe.
108. Jason kills them.
109. She escaped from Jason and the muggers.
110. The police.
111. "Ok, take your best shot."
112. Beheaded with a punch
113. Julius' head.
114. Rennie
115. The police officer.
116. Rennie
117. Because Rennie crashed head on into a wall and the car catches on fire and then explodes.
118. Sean, Rennie and Charles McCullough
119. Collen Van Deusen
120. Her uncle pushed her in Crystal Lake when she was little and she didn't know how to swim, and the boy Jason pulled her under.
121. No
122. Charles McCullough
123. Charles McCullough
124. Charles McCullough
125. Sean and Rennie
126. Sean and Rennie
127. The emergency brake.
128. Jason

129.   Rennie
130.   The gang members boom box.
131.   "Hey man, your dead meat man."
132.   He lifts his hockey mask up so they can see his face.
133.   Yes, It's cool man.   It's cool.
134.   Dallas
135.   Throws him against a wall.
136.   "Welcome to New York"
137.   Toxic waste
138.   Midnight
139.   Bashed in the head with a wrench.
140.   "You didn't get me in the lake and you sure are not going to get me now."
141.   Toxic waste from a can.
142.   Yes
143.   22 stories tall
144.   Rennie's dog, Toby.
145.   Timothy Burr Mirkovich
146.   Toby
147.   Gang Bangers #1 and #2.
148.   The white boxer was originally killed by a dart in each eye. The producer was forced to cut it because it was deemed to graphic. It was replaced. By two hot rocks in his stomach
149.   Jim - impaled with a spear gun.
Suzie Donaldson - stabbed with a spear in the chest.
JJ - bashed in the head with her electric guitar.
Boxer - hot sauna rock in the chest.
Tamara - stabbed with a mirror shard.
Jim Carlson - harpooned in back.
Admiral Robertson - throat slit with a machete.
Eva - strangled.
Crewmember - accidentally shot by Wayne.
Wayne - electrocuted on a control panel.
Miles - impaled on a deck post.
Deck hand - axed in the back
Seven anonymous students - left to die on a burning ship.
Gang Banger #1 - stabbed through the back with his own syringe.

Gang Banger #2 - bashed and scalded on a steam pipe.
Julius - Jason beheads him with a punch.
Cop - dragged into an alley and killed off screen.
Collen Van Deusen - immolated in a burning car.
Charles McCullough - drowned in a barrel of sewage.
A Diner worker - thrown against a wall (unconfirmed).
Sanitation worker - bashed in the head with a wrench.

150. Julius'
151. Jim
152. Lady Drifter
153. Eva and Tamara
154. Charles McCullough
155. Canada
156. Rob Hedden
157. A boy
158. Randolph Cheveldave
159. (20)
160. (2)
161. Rennie and Sean
162. He drowned in a flood of toxic waste.
163. 96 minutes
164. 1989
165. Car accident
166. Yes
167. Crazy Ralph (Parts 1 and 2) and Abel (Part 3)
168. Harry Manfredini
169. Paramount Pictures
170. A little less than 15 million.
171. Yes
172. New Line Cinema
173. Throw up
174. No
175. Seven and a half weeks to film.
176. He drank 2 pitchers of water right before they filmed that scene.
177. No

Answers for Jason Goes To Hell: The Final Friday the 13th Trivia Questions:

A. Matching:

1. D
2. A
3. B
4. F
5. G
6. M
7. T
8. J
9. S
10. C
11. E
12. H
13. L
14. O
15. Q
16. N
17. P
18. T
19. V
20. R
21. K
22. CC
23. U
24. Z
25. X
26. BB
27. AA
28. W

B. Answers to the Questions:

29.   Diana

30.   An FBI attack has killed Jason, they blew him up.

31.   The coroner

32.   (3)

33.   Jessica, Steven and Stephanie

34.   (21)

35.   A Waitress

36.   Kane Hodder

37.   Corner's fingers through skull.

38.   Sean S. Cunningham

39.   Black

40.   The Voorhees house.

41.   Yes

42.   Red

43.   The light goes out

44.   White

45.   Jason Voorhees

46.   Her own blood.

47.   Creighton Duke

48.   A little bit.

49.   Blue

50.   Yes

51.   Black with blue tie

52   230 or 240

53   Yes

54   Double the size of a normal heart.

55   Examines it first and then eats it.

56   He is possessed by Jason's spirit.

57   Lemeckis Pizza

58   He is killed. Autopsy probe in the back of the neck, face pushed through a metal grating.

59   They are also killed #1 - pencil through his spinal cord and #2 - coroner's finger's through his skull.

60.   83 confirmed murders plus 5 more from morgue to Crystal Lake.

61.   Pamela Sue Parker Voorhees and Elias Voorhees.

62.   Lemonade
63.   No one has ever seen the true Jason Voorhees.
64.   Orange
65.   500 grand
66.   Diana
67.   Black
68.   She wanted to tell him about Jessica's baby that is his.
69.   Voorhees Burger and a side of Jason fingers (which was the special of the day)
70.   11 p.m.
71.   The joke was going to Crystal Lake to smoke dope and having a little premarital sex and getting slaughtered (Jason was supposedly dead).
72.   (3)
73.   It is broken.
74.   They were torn down.
75.   Yellow
76.   Full
77.   Nothing
78.   Red and green plaid blouse.
79.   A condom packet.
80.   Silver
81.   Tango was a little dog that Diana fed.
82.   Red gingham
83.   Going to use the bathroom of course outdoors.
84.   Head slammed in a car door.
85.   Steven's
86.   (4)
87.   Diana's daughter, Diana was Jason's sister.
88.   Jason Voorhees
89.   No
90.   She was killed.
91.   Killed with a straight razor.
92.   Josh
93.   Her daughter, Jessica.
94.   Diana shoots Josh.
95.   Stephanie is Jessica's daughter.
96.   Jessica's baby is a Voorhees.

97.   Vicki
98.   Vicki
99.   Steven
100. Steven
101. For harassing Diana
102. They can destroy Jason or through them he will be reborn again only through a Voorhees can he be reborn and only in the hands of a Voorhees may he die.
103. Randy
104. Vicki
105. Disappears, he melts away.
106. In the store room
107. 8,C
108. A book that has symbols in it and skeletons in it.
109. Robert Campbell
110. The lights go out.
111. A shirt, a hammer and then in the car a flash light.
112. In the garage.
113. He gets possessed by Jason' and later shot in head, run over with car, impaled on a barbecue skewer.
114. Because he is possessed by Jason's spirit.
115. Yells at Steven, hits and punches Steven and pushes Steven out of the car and leaves him on the side of the road and drives away.
116. Randy is Steven's best friend.
117. Robert Campbell, who is Jessica's new boyfriend.
118. Because Steven stole his service revolver and locked him in a cell.
119. Josh who was possessed by Jason's spirit
120. Eight times at the police station and two more times at the diner.
121. They get killed, their heads knocked together.
122. The Sheriff, Sheriff Landers.
123. Jessica called the sheriff.
124. Ward worked at the Diner and is Joey B's son.
125. Joey B, she was slugged by Jessica.
126. He kills her, burned to death on a deep fryer and grill.
127. He gets killed, arm broken, falls dead through the diner doors.

128.   She gets killed, face bashed in.

129.   Impaled on a barbecue skewer, head crushed.

130.   To get Jessica to come to the Voorhees house and listen to him.

131.   Fancy Glass Window

132.   Jessica

133.   Ward

134.   The Voorhees house.

135.   Sheriff Landers.

136.   He tries to possess the baby as Jason.

137.   His dead sister, Diana's

138.   Randy

139.   The dagger falls through a crack in the floor that is under a dresser.

140.   He is killed by Jason.

141.   (3)

142.   He gets stabbed with the family dagger by his niece, Jessica and then is taken to Hell by demons.

143.   (3)

144.   Four or five or more.

145.   Freddy Krueger

146.   The cut scene are:

    1. Footage in the first diner scene that expands on the relationships of the Sheriff and Diana, Steven and Randy.

    2. A scene where Creighton Duke is brought in for looking in the morgue cabinet that once contained Diana's body. Duke tells Landers: "Trying to steal the body, but someone got to it before I could." Duke is locked up.

    3. Scene of David having his head bashed against a faucet.

    4. Detailed pencil killing of FBI Agent #1 and detailed fingers in the skull killing FBI Agent #2.

147.   Bloopers:

    1. When the Lady FBI agent pulls up to the house it is daytime, when she opens the door to go into the house it is nighttime.

    2. Steven, Jessica, Robert, and Jason who has Josh's body are all in the Voorhees house. They fight a little bit and Steven ends up putting Jessica in the car. They see Robert who is

now possessed by Jason and run him over. His waste is the place that received the most damage. It was all bloody and torn up. Then Robert goes to the police station and his waste looks like nothing happened to it at all.

3. When Steve and Duke are in jail, Duke breaks two of Steven's fingers. Then in the rest of the movie, there is clearly nothing wrong with his fingers.

4. Jason already has his first body the coroner. Then he takes the body of Josh. When he has him strapped to the table he puts some shaving cream on him. The amount of cream he has on him gets bigger and smaller each time the camera goes off Josh and back on he has a different amount on him.

5. When the morgue attendant is inspecting Jason's blown up body, he is wearing a watch on his left wrist, but while he is eating the heart the watch disappears and then reappears over and over.

6. The mailbox sign reads "Vorhees" it should be "Voorhees".

7. In the scene where the corner is Jason in the morgue, in one shot he has gloves on and in the next shot he is missing them.

8. In the very beginning where the FBI agent is running away from Jason, and from one scene to the next, she goes from shoes to no shoes about five or six times.

9. Jessica's baby is very young and without hair in an early scene but later the baby is older and with a full head of hair.

10. When the female FBI Agent falls off the balcony in the first scene, she lands on a coffee table, clearly knocking the legs of the table out from under it. In the next shot, she is lying on the table and the table's legs are still under it.

11. After Jason kills Diana, and the Sheriff finds Steven with the body, he doesn't have hardly any blood on his jeans. Later at the police station, his pants are covered with blood.

12. At an earlier point in the same scene, when Steven impales Josh with the fireplace poker, Josh stumbles very slowly

toward the window, but in the next shot, he is moving with enough force to move across the room and shatter through a window.

13. When Steven is fighting with Randy by the police car, you can clearly see in one shot that he has his gun in the back reflection of Jason stays still.

14. Jason is supposed to have only one "good" eye, but in Josh's reflection of Jason you can see Kane Hodder's eye looking out of Jason's bad eye socket.

15. When Steven impales Josh with the fireplace poker, Josh starts to stumble very slowly toward the window, but in the next shot, he is moving with enough force to move across the room and shatter through a window.

16. The blood on Robert's face drips out the right side of his mouth as the "hellbaby" is passed into him, but when he stands up it is on the left side.

17. In the scene where Steven carries Jessica out of her mother's house after punching Robert, you can see a cameraman in the passenger window of the car as the couple gets into it.

18. You can see a reflection of Robert in the car's hood when he is grabbing at Steven though the driver's side window. Since he is possessed by Jason's spirit, there should be a reflection of Jason instead.

19. When Steven is fighting with Randy by the police car, you can clearly see in one shot that he has his gun in the back of his pants, but later he pulls the gun out of the front of his jeans.

20. When Steven is being led down the corridor in handcuffs, and sees Jessica in trouble; he jumps up and passes his arms under his legs, but if you look closely you can see that it is just string between his arms and he pulls his hands a lot wider apart than real handcuffs would go.

21. When Jessica leaves the restaurant to go to the Voorhees house she has large stripes of blood on her neck, when she gets out of the truck they are gone, and they reappear when she is talking to Creighton Duke.

22. In the first shot of the pole in Duke's leg it is very bloody, but in the next shot when he is yelling to Jessica, there is a noticeable lack of blood.

23. If Randy was possessed by Jason; why did he talk normally to Jessica? Also why did Randy look fine when all the other host bodies become all nasty and zombie - looking?

24. After being "reborn" through Diana, it is rather odd that Jason comes out fully clothed and with his mask on.

25. When Jason is pulled into the ground his mask is securely on his head, but then his mask is shown lying on the ground at the end.

26. At the end of Part 8 Jason drowns in the toxic waste and turns into a boy again, but in Part 9 he is fully grown and with a mask which was destroyed in the waste from Part 8 (which it turn was destroyed in Part 7). Explanation: The boy was another of Rennie's hallucinations. Jason washed out to sea, along with his slightly melted mask.

27. When the FBI agent gets to the house, you can see the sun is just setting, but then there is bright midday sun when she enters the cabin, and then total darkness when she goes to the shed.

28. When Agent Marcus puts the light bulb into the socket, the dead one has been placed on the ladder. She then proceeds to fold up the ladder and lean it against the wall, leaving us with a disappearing light bulb.

29. When Agent Marcus hears a noise, she slips something into her towel. The script this was a gun, so why didn't she use it on Jason? Is that what caused the blood on the front of her towel when she fell?

30. When Agent Marcus falls off the balcony and lands on the coffee table, the legs are clearly knocked out to the side, but in the next shot the table's legs are tucked under the table top.

31. When Agent Marcus is running away from Jason, from one scene to the next she goes from shoes to no shoes, to shoes to no shoes about five or six times. Also her towel

was sure securely attached as she sprinted through the forest.

32. At the ambush site, it is unclear as to where all the FBI agents are shooting from, making it look like they are in a circle surrounding Jason. If they were really in a circle, then they would be shooting at each other as well as Jason.

33. The bomb that is dropped actually explodes behind Jason, then there is a pause before Jason actually explodes. It is also unclear as to where this "bomb" was dropped from so precisely as to not injure the FBI agents.

34. You can see that Jason's detached head didn't really fall from the sky, but it was rather obviously dropped from right above the camera. You can tell, because there is a piece of straw that is visible at the top of the screen that is attached to the fake head and it is held there a moment before it is dropped.

35. When the coroner is inspecting Jason's body he is wearing a watch on his left wrist, but while he is eating the heart the watch disappears but returns after he is possessed.

36. When the coroner sees Jason's heart beating, from shot to shot he has a little blood, then a lot, and then just a little again, but when he goes to actually eat the heart there is a lot of black liquid on his face.

37. On the American Case File show, they show pictures of the coroners that were killed. The picture of the assistant coroner is just a still from the previous scene.

38. When Deborah and her guy start to make love in the tent, she throws the condom a side, and then the coroner steps on a condom outside. Explanation: It's not the same condom, folks! Always be prepared with more than one.

39. When the coroner runs toward the car to slam Edna's head in the door, Josh doesn't seem to notice even though he is facing in the coroner's direction.

40. The amount of shaving cream on Josh's face changes from shot to shot in the Voorhees' house, and if you look closely you will see his moustache is already gone before the coroner shaves it.

41. Jessica's baby is very young and without hair in an early scene, but later the baby is older and with a full head of hair.
42. Before being impaled with the poker, Josh lifts his head to look into the mirror in the living room but the reflection of Jason stays still.
43. When Steven stabs Josh with the poker you can see clearly that it goes all the way through him, but later in the movie when Josh goes to posses Robert, there is no blood on his front or on his back.
44. The blood on Robert's face drips out the right side of his mouthy as the "hellbaby" is passed into him, but when he stands up it is on the left side.
45. In the scene where Steven carries Jessica out of her mother's house after punching Robert, you can see a cameraman in the passenger window of the car as the couple gets into it.
46. You can see a reflection of Robert in the car's hood when he is grabbing at Steven through the driver's side window. Since he is possessed by Jason's spirit, there should be a reflection of Jason instead.
47. When the policeman at the end of the hall is shot in the head, the bullet "hole" just looks like paint because of the glimmer of light and the distinctiveness of the forehead.
48. When Jessica leaves the restaurant to go to the Voorhees house she has large stripes of blood on her neck, when she gets out of the truck they are gone, and they reappear when she is talking to Creighton Duke.
49. If Randy was possessed by Jason, why did he talk normally to Jessica? Also whey did randy look fine when all the other host bodies became all nasty and zombie-looking.
50. After being "reborn" through Diana, it is rather odd that Jason comes out fully clothed and with is mask on.
51. When Jason is pulled into the ground his mask is securely on his head, but then his mask is shown lying on the ground at the end.

148. The "safe-sex kills" scene was added while shooting an extra three days for some exposition shots. It appears the audience wanted more nudity.
149. Joey B's
150. "All Persons Entering This Area Subject to Security Search"
151. Thirteen burst of light comes from Jason and into the coroner.
152. Youngstown, Ohio
153. Federal Morgue
154. Here is everyone and how they were killed:
    Coroner - eats Jason's heart, dies and becomes possessed.
    Coroner's Assistant - Autopsy probe in the back of the neck, face pushed through a metal grating.
    FBI Agent #1 - Pencil through his spinal cord.
    FBI Agent # 2 - Coroner's fingers through his skull.
    Alexis - Slashed up with a straight razor.
    Deborah - Stabbed through the back with a barbed wire spike, ripped in half.
    Luke - Head crushed off-screen.
    Edna - Head slammed in car door.
    Josh - Possessed by Jason, shot in head and impaled with poker, later melts away.
    Diana - Knife sharpening pole in back.
    Robert Campbell - Possessed by Jason, later shot in head, run over with car, impaled on a barbecue skewer.
    Officer Ryan - Head bashed against a locker.
    Officer Mark and Officer Brian - Heads bashed together.
    Ward - Arm broken, falls dead through the diner doors.
    Shelby - Burned to death on a deep fat fryer and grill.
    Joey B - Face bashed in.
    Vicki - Impaled on a barbecue skewer, head crushed.
    Randy - Possessed by Jason, later his neck is severed with a machete.
    Creighton Duke - Crushed to death by Jason.

155. Double the size of a normal heart.
156. He told her that she is the only living relative that can destroy Jason for good.
157. Crystal Lake

158. (34)
159. Knife sharpening pole in the back.
160. (11)
161. Hockey masks
162. Voorhees Burgers and Jason fingers (the burgers were shaped like hockey masks)(hamburgers and fries)
163. The coroner, Josh, Robert Campbell and Randy
164. Yes. But not by Jason, Jessica stabs him with the family dagger.
165. Adam Marcus.
166. He put some shaving cream on Josh and shaved him.
167. To her daughter Jessica.
168. Steven's
169. Josh
170. The Voorhees house.
171. Robert Campbell
172. The Voorhees house in a closet.
173. Yes
174. Yes
175. (1)
176. Luke the boy camper was killed off screen by the coroner who was possessed by Jason's spirit.
177. July 20, 1992
178. Sean S. Cunningham
179. Kane Hodder
180. Adam Marcus
181. Harry Manfredini
182. Yes
183. New Line Cinema
184. 1993
185. A pizza
186. FBI Agent #2
187. "I don't think so."
188. A machete
189. Right hand
190. In the back of the head.
191. A little girl in a pink dress sticking a hotdog through a doughnut.

192.   American Case File
193.   Jason is dead 2 for 1 burger sale.
194.   Diana
195.   Yes
196.   Right side of head.
197.   A bounty hunter.
198.   This is truly sick.
199.   Steven and Josh (when he was possessed by Jason's spirit)
200.   A fire poker
201.   I have your baby, come to the Voorhees house alone.
202.   (4)
203.   Fairfield 33 and Westport 43
204.   Twice the Life, made in the USA.
205.   60 Watt
206.   The door closes and the light turns off.
207.   Yes
208.   Butterflies
209.   Yes
210.   Their heads were bashed together.
211.   A grenade
212.   yes
213.   A machete
214.   Right
215.   40- day schedule
216.   Starting on July 20, 1992
217.   Yes
218.   FBI Agent # 2
219.   Yes
220.   6' 7"
221.   6' 5"
222.   (138)
223. (106)
224. Bride of Chucky (at the police station locked up)
225. Yes
226. Jason X
227. April 13, 2001
228. Yes

About the Author

She has been a Horror movie fan for many years. She thought it would be fun to compose a simple trivia book on horror movies for entertainment. She has on different occasions attended horror movie conventions, which gave her opportunities to meet and talk with many actors, directors and special make-up effects people who gave her a closer insight into the movies. It is her hope that this trivia book will be challenging and entertaining for the many fans and followers of the *Friday the 13th* movies.

Best of luck, and let the excitement begin.

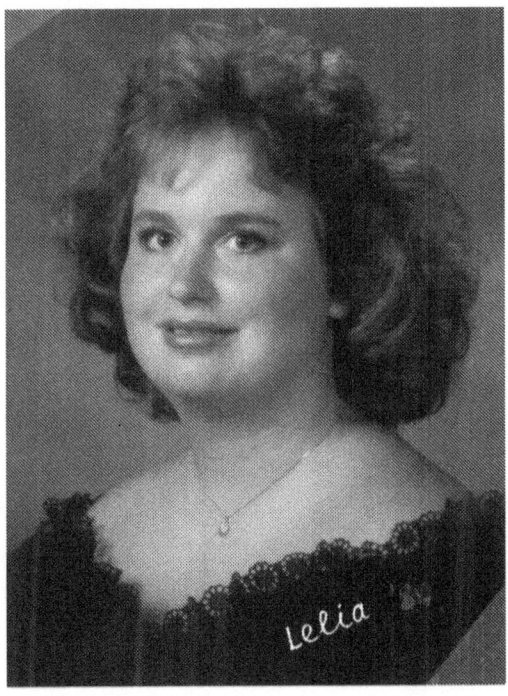

www.ingramcontent.com/pod-product-compliance
Lightning Source LLC
Chambersburg PA
CBHW030322290526
45785CB00001B/471